Did You Ever Wonder What's Happening at Mass?

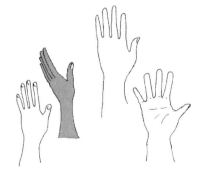

Did You Ever Wonder What's Happening at Mass?

Loretta Therese Brady

with Illustrations by Anthony Keating

All references to the Bible have been taken from the New American Bible Translation 1970-1991.

All references to the Vatican II documents have been taken from the Vatican website. www.vatican.va (See Resource Library, Ecumenical Councils, Second Vatican Council, Constitutions, *Sacrosanctum Concilium*)

Cover photo of Basilica Shrine of St. Mary, Wilmington NC
by Loretta Therese Brady
Design assist by Noemi, Kevin and Flor Hernandez
and FLUX AV of Wilmington NC

Copyright © 2020 Loretta Therese Brady
ISBN 978-1-09833-363-8

nourishyourspirit2020@gmail.com

CONTENTS

Why and how this book came to be:

Author's Note

IN September of 2010 a lovely, friendly young woman walked into an RCIA gathering asking: "Is this the group where I learn all about what's going on with Catholics?" How refreshing! I was already happy to be part of the team facilitating RCIA (the Rite of Christian Initiation of Adults). This is the journey some Catholics travel with those who are interested in becoming Catholic. Now after hearing Dottie Carter's opening question I was thrilled to be a part of this particular group. Dottie quickly became my favorite "newbie" and has remained to this day a very favorite friend. The sunshine of her spirit and frank openness cut through all the churchy formality, getting right to the heart of the matter every time she spoke.

One day when we were discussing the Mass Dottie asked: "You know at the beginning of the Mass why does the priest look like he's smelling the tablecloth?" Her question and the way she framed it totally stopped me in my tracks. It caused what I like to call "a train wreck in my mind." All my assumptions that those attending Mass understand what's happening tumbled down in a heap creating a whole new formation in my mind. If that one little gesture was picked up as a strange curiosity by Dottie, just imagine all that is misunderstood or not understood at all. That one question continued to work on rearranging the previous order of my mind.

I began to be inspired to look at every single prayer and reading and gesture of the Mass, questioning why these were parts of the Mass. One thing I encountered along the way is that many people who had been raised and educated in the Catholic culture had the same kind of questions that Dottie had asked. In various polls taken today about religious involvement the guide for who is Catholic is always "Do they go to Mass?" It seemed to me that if that was the one thing that "practicing Catholics" do regularly isn't it sad that so many of us don't know what we're doing or why.

A young mother who had gone through 12 years of Catholic education and now has two little ones of her own told me that there were many parts of the Mass where she had no idea what was going on. Sheila told me that Mass for her was hoping her two little ones would not break out in mutiny before the Eucharistic Prayer was over. She humorously said that the meaning of the bells ringing meant for her "I made it. We're almost home." I wanted to offer answers of meaning to her and Dottie and anyone else who felt clueless but answers spelled out in the same simple direct way that Dottie had asked her questions.

A short time after Dottie had posed her questions I asked the pastor at our parish, St. Therese in Wrightsville Beach, North Carolina, if I could place a series of articles in the bulletin each week. The idea was to ask a Dottie-question and then direct those who were interested to go to the parish website to find the answer.

Our pastor, Fr. Joe Vetter, gave his usual supportive encouragement: "That's good, Loretta. Go ahead." No questions asked. Fr. Joe Vetter had a marvelous grace he poured out on everyone. He empowered people to take the lead. With Father Joe's "Go ahead" you always got an immediate sense of his respect for you and your idea as well as his encouragement. When I shared with him that I was thinking of doing this book he said (yes, you guessed it) "That's good Loretta. Go ahead." He even agreed to edit it! Fr. John McGee OSFS, pastor of Immaculate Conception Parish in Wilmington generously completed this editing after Father Joe had returned Home. So we moved from Dottie's questions to the bulletin & website articles and now into a book.

This describes why this book was written. My explanation of the inspiration and encouragement I received wouldn't be complete though unless I also mentioned one other person, Father John Gillespie. When I came to North Carolina he was the first pastor I met when I attended St. Mary Parish in Wilmington. I've never known anyone who has read more books. Simply put, he's a lifelong learner. Along with a great desire to learn is his mission to teach. He's always teaching his parishioners something new.

A favorite approach of Father John Gillespie's is to come in front of the People before he vests for Mass and describe just one simple part of the

Mass explaining why we include it in our liturgy. By the end of a few seasons the People have all learned the whole Mass. I experienced firsthand the positive effect of his wise approach to teaching something so complex. That's how I learned so much about the Mass. You might say he is the ghost writer of this book. It was his concept of teaching just one part at a time as well as what he taught that made such a strong impression on me. His approach is what I had in mind from the time I began to gather all the "whys" for Dottie.

Just like Father John Gillespie, I offer you one piece at a time until the total picture emerges as a whole. Let me suggest as you take up this book that you only read one section at a time—maybe one a week. Then attend a Mass and focus on that one part. In less than a year you'll have read about the whole Mass and, I'm pretty sure, you'll find that participating at Mass is much more understandable and fulfilling. Then you, along with me, will be very grateful to Dottie, Sheila, Father Joe and Father John.

—LORETTA THERESE BRADY 2020

1. *In what ways does the Mass resemble a family reunion?*

GATHER, TELL STORIES, SHARE A MEAL, WISH US WELL ON OUR WAY

ISN'T this the flow of most every family holiday gathering? It's the natural way that families meet and greet and spend special times together.

Then think again about this flow. Isn't this also the natural way we come together each time we assemble for Mass?

We gather and celebrate our unity as a family in signs and symbols, in prayers and song.

Then we sit to listen while some among us tell the stories of our ancestors in the faith. And we respond to these special messages from God in prayer and song, hoping to absorb this wisdom for use in our own lives.

After certain preparations in which we all take some special part, we share a meal as one family. Then we take the time to fully appreciate this most amazing meal that has nourished us.

Finally with a renewed spirit, we are sent on our way to bring the grace and joy of this gathering to everyone we meet. We're sent on mission.

Over the centuries the Church has carefully guarded these traditions, first developed among our Hebrew ancestors. The earliest Christians began to meld both the Hebrew Passover meal with the New Covenant messages of Jesus. Down through the ages of history, cultures and customs were added, deleted, obscured then clarified. Yet in each era the flow of the event always remained the same: Gather, Listen, Share, Mission.

When you meet up with your family at various events, take note of the flow at all these celebrations. And as you assemble for Mass during this same time, notice how the flow of that most special celebration resembles your family get-togethers. Not so surprising, since we are all God's family.

2. *What are we supposed to do during this event?*

Our Roles at the Gathering

THIS isn't meant to be a passive, receptive event but rather one filled with meaningful interaction from all of us. When we gather to celebrate the Eucharist we're aware that there are several people who take on specific roles to make this event special. The Priest is the Presider, the one who presides over our gathering. He is at times referred to as being *in persona christi*, acting "in the person of Christ" who makes all things holy. Then sometimes there is a Deacon, and there are altar servers, lectors, choir members, ushers, and the eucharistic ministers. Some others fulfill roles that we don't often see like the sacristan who prepares the things for the celebration of the Eucharist and checks to see that everyone is present and in place. There are also those at some of our churches who serve to see that the altar, the flowers, all of the sanctuary and other parts of our church inspire us with beauty as we gather to pray.

The music and liturgy director does many things throughout the week to prepare for our celebrations. Music must be chosen according to the liturgical season, the particular Mass readings of the day within the guidelines of the Church and in the culture of the congregation. Many of these people whom we call liturgical ministers, especially the choir members and the lectors, also practice their parts beforehand. The Priest spends time preparing a suitable homily for each particular Mass.

What about the rest of us? We've gradually learned mostly all the cues for the stand up/sit down parts we play. But why do we do that at all? Briefly, we stand to be together in community, to show our active participation and to offer respectful praise to God. We sit when it's appropriate for us to listen and be receptive. And we kneel at times of serious reflection and personal meditation. But is that all there is for us to do?

Fifty years ago the deliberations at the Second Vatican Council addressed this question and developed the document entitled *The Constitution on the Sacred Liturgy* which was approved by 2,147 bishops. This document stated: *In the restoration and promotion of the sacred liturgy, this full and active participation by all the people is the aim to be considered before all else. (from Sacrosanctum Concilium, #14, paragraph 2)*

Quoting further from this document gives some idea of its invitation and challenge to us.

> *Mother Church earnestly desires that all the faithful should be led to that fully conscious, and active participation in liturgical celebrations which is demanded by the very nature of the liturgy. (SC, #14, paragraph 1)*

Let's start looking at this challenging invitation with one idea first. We're told that God is present at each Eucharistic Liturgy (Mass) in four distinct ways. Most of us would identify one manifestation of God's presence as being in the Body and Blood of Christ. Some may also rightly point out that the Scripture readings are the word of God and therefore signify another way God is present at Mass. Earlier in this section it was mentioned that the Priest stands in place of Christ, so there is the third way we experience God's presence.

The fourth manifestation of God's presence is in the Assembly -- yes US, the People. In gathering together we represent the body of Christ, God with us. As we read in the gospel of Matthew, "Where two or three are gathered together in my name, there I am in your midst." We together represent God in this world, bringing the message of love to everyone, building the Kingdom of God in the here and now. And in order to do the work of God we need to be supported, instructed, as well as nourished and encouraged.

As the above mentioned Vatican Council II document states the sacred liturgy, . . . is the primary and indispensable source from which the faithful are to derive the true Christian spirit; *(SC, #14, paragraph 2)*

It is by participating in the sacred liturgy, the Mass, that we'll gain the courage and strength needed to do the work God asks of us. So, we as members of the Assembly need to learn about the prayers, signs, symbols and gestures. We need to know what they mean, what they're saying, what we're saying, as we go through all these together. What are we saying to God and to each other during the liturgy? And why?

As a seasoned actor plays a role in a drama, it isn't enough that the lines are memorized. The actor has to become part of the story, get into the character, feel the feelings of the person. The actor has to prepare both in mind and in heart for this activity and we in the Assembly are much more than actors in a drama. Through our Baptism we've each assumed a crucial part in the creation of God's kingdom of love on earth.

Once again, let's look at what the Vatican Council II document states: *Such participation by the Christian people as a chosen race, a royal priesthood, a holy nation, a redeemed people (1 Pet. 2:9; cf. 2:4-5), is their right and duty by reason of their baptism. SC, #14, (paragraph 1)*

By our Baptism we each are anointed to be priest, prophet and king – as priest, to make all things around us holy – as prophet, to speak God's truth to all – and as king, to be benevolent caretakers and protectors of each other. That's a tall order. Where can we get the courage and the strength to do that every day? This is what can come to us if we fully participate in the Eucharistic Liturgy.

The questions and answers that follow here offer an opportunity to learn more about what happens at Mass and how we as a family of believers can fulfill our liturgical ministry as members of the Assembly, gaining the necessary strength and courage to be fully alive Christians.

3. When does the Mass begin?

THE INTRODUCTORY RITE

LET'S talk about what's involved in this very beginning introduction of the Mass. First of all, the word Rite is used in describing various parts of Catholic liturgy. It refers to the prayers and actions that are standardized procedures used repeatedly whenever we gather. The purpose of the Introductory Rite is to gather the faithful together as one holy People, the Body of Christ, united in worship. A group of individuals comes together as a unified body, the Assembly, to respond to God's call. This is why The Introductory Rite is sometimes referred to as The Gathering. It prepares the Assembly to listen to the word of God and to celebrate the Eucharist together.

The actual preparation starts long before we even arrive at church. It begins at that point when each one of us makes the decision to gather for Mass. Then, while still at home, we prepare ourselves by the clothes we choose to wear, the donation of money or food we plan to bring with us and perhaps by reading the Scripture passages that will be part of the Mass for the day.

When we arrive, we greet others whom we meet on the way into the church. Often there are fellow parishioners who officially greet us at the door. Many people sign themselves with holy water from the fonts at the doorway. This is a special custom which reminds us of our Baptism which claimed us as children of God. Another custom which some choose is to genuflect, kneel on one knee, before moving to sit down. This is to show special respect for the Eucharist present in the tabernacle. If the Eucharist is in the tabernacle the red light, the sanctuary lamp next to it will be glowing. Finally, it's also a custom to bow toward the altar before sitting. This is most appropriate because the altar represents God. It is where we will place our offerings in the hands of God. It is both the altar of sacrifice and the table of thanksgiving. Throughout the Mass the Priest and several liturgical ministers will bow before the altar showing special respect.

In the pre-Vatican Council II description of the Mass it was said that the Mass would begin *"when the priest is ready."* Since the Vatican Council II the description now reads that the Mass begins *"when the people have gathered."* The vision was widened to encompass the entire People of God. We are called as one Body of Christ to act in union with one another for the common good of all and for the whole world. The Priest is *in persona Christi capitis,* "in the person of Christ as Head." In liturgical notes the Priest is referred to as the Presider. We gather together to express our love for one another, to give thanks to God and to give ourselves as one in the offering of the Mass.

The following are the parts of the Mass that together are referred to as the Introductory Rite:

Entrance, Sign of the Cross, Greeting, Penitential Act,
Gloria, Collect

4. Why does the Priest look like he's smelling the altar linen?

THE ENTRANCE

THIS first part of the Introductory Rite is where we see that unusual look-ing gesture the priest makes as he leans into the altar. This is only one part of the Entrance ceremony. The Entrance is first of all a chant written for every day of the Church year. This may be said or sung. That's why this first part of the liturgy is referred to as the Entrance Chant. There are many guidelines given for the liturgist or music minister about how to use this. The most common choice is to use another liturgical chant or song which the whole Assembly can sing together. That's why this initial part of the Mass is also referred to as the Entrance Song. Because it serves to gather the Assembly and open the liturgy. It is also sometimes called the Gathering Song or the Opening Hymn. In all cases it should reflect the particular liturgy of the day, the liturgical season and feast.

When the Assembly sings together this helps to foster unity. We are not only singing together we are literally breathing together. This has a physi-cally unifying effect which helps us to connect not only with each other but with God as the Breath of Life.

As all gathered sing together, the procession begins. This is a very signifi-cant and meaningful event as it reminds us of so many spiritual journeys. We recall our Hebrew ancestors in faith who journeyed from slavery to the Promised Land. We think of all Christians whose lives actually are spiri-tual journeys, answering God's call one day at a time throughout all our years here. We're remembering too that we are pilgrims on a journey Home.

The procession itself feels like it is the start of the Mass, yet the procession actually started as each of us made our way to the church. Each time some-one entered the church the Assembly became more and more full until finally the liturgical ministers and the Priest walking up the aisle make the gathering complete. This procession in a symbolic way brings us all up the aisle to the altar to celebrate together.

The procession is led by the cross bearer who holds up before us the sign of our faith, the cross. This is our first statement of faith together: We belong to Jesus Christ who suffered and died for our sins, who rose gloriously from the dead proclaiming victory over death for all of us. Belonging to Jesus Christ means that we believe in what he taught us, what he showed us about how to live, and we've promised to bring this message to all the world. That is what the cross at the head of our procession is saying for all of us. It symbolizes our act of faith.

The cross bearer is followed by the other liturgical ministers, the altar servers and the Priest who will preside for us. One of the lectors, will be holding high the Book of the Gospels to announce that God is in our midst. God is present with us at Mass in four ways: in the Assembly, the word of God, the Priest and soon in the Eucharist.

As the procession reaches the front of the church, the cross bearer places the cross in a prominent position, the servers bow before the altar and take their places at the side. The lector processes to the altar and places the Book of the Gospels on the altar in a position of honor for all of us to see. The Book of the Gospels containing the word of God is one of two ways we will be nourished by God during the Mass. The Book is positioned on the altar in the same place where the bread and wine will be later. This reminds us that God gives us our daily bread in two special ways, through his word of revelation and through his body and blood.

Following the lector the Priest processes to the altar, which represents the hands of God, and kisses it. Finally, an answer to the initial question of what the Priest does at the altar at the beginning of Mass that looks like he's smelling the altar linen. His gesture is what is known as *reverencing the altar*. At some special feasts the altar is also sprinkled with holy water or incensed. The altar is the central focus for the entire worship service. There are relics of saints embedded in the altar. This helps us to remember those holy ones who also once celebrated the Mass and now have gone before us. The altar servers, ministers and Priest all now take their appropriate places.

5. *Why does everything Catholic begin with the Sign of the Cross?*

The Sign of the Cross

THE Priest and, along with him, the entire Assembly make the Sign of the Cross. The Priest traces a cross on his body, from head to heart, from left shoulder to right shoulder as he says the words:

"In the name of the Father, and of the Son and of the Holy Spirit"

The Faithful follow in this gesture-prayer and answer

"Amen."

What we once did individually as we entered the church, we now do with everyone gathered together. We are no longer alone but with others who also believe in and trust God in the same way we do. Why do we sign ourselves with this prayer to the Trinity: Father, Son and Holy Spirit? We're claiming that we believe and are about to worship in God's name. This gesture-prayer reminds us of God's love in sending Jesus into our midst. We're also remembering that Jesus' suffering and death on the cross has overcome the powers of sin and death. And we're acknowledging the Spirit which Jesus promised is with us now. From the day of our Baptism and onward we belong to God: Father, Son and Holy Spirit and in this we're united with our fellow believers.

The Sign of the Cross expresses the central event of Christian faith. Signing our body not only claims us for Christ but signifies that everything about our very person is changed forever through our belief in Christ. This gesture is itself a prayer, even without words. It suggests to us the sacred mystery that is to come as we pray the Mass.

The words, *"In the name of the Father, and of the Son, and of the Holy Spirit"* is what Jesus said to his apostles as he sent them forth to baptize all nations with these words. Think of this: these are the first words you heard as a Catholic. These are the words that were said over you as the cross was traced on your forehead at Baptism. This is the mark of God upon us. Every time we make the Sign of the Cross and say the words Father, Son and Holy Spirit, we are reliving and renewing our Baptism. It seems appropriate to begin to pray the Mass with this sign and these words. They signify our entrance once again into the mystery of Jesus' passion, death and resurrection for our salvation. And when we say *"Amen"* we're choosing once again to go deeper into this sacred mystery.

6. *Why do the People and the Priest have to remind each other that God is with us? Don't they already know that?*

AS we go through each day at work or school or home, shopping for groceries, watching sports, playing sports or exercising, having lunch or dinner with friends, are we actually thinking that God is with us? Probably not. But Jesus said in Matthew 28:20 "I will be with you always."

So, as we gather to meet God together we start by reminding ourselves of this phenomenal gift: God is with us – always!

Following the Sign of the Cross we offer a special spiritual greeting to one another.

Priest: *"The Lord be with you."*

People: *"And with your Spirit."*

Two small phrases and yet they say so much. These phrases can be heard throughout the Hebrew and Christian Scriptures, the Old and New Testaments of the Bible.

In the book of Judges we read that an angel appeared to Gideon calling him to save his people. The angel said *"The Lord is with you, O champion."* Gideon was told, be calm, be at peace, the Lord will help you save your people. In accepting his calling Gideon built an altar naming it the altar of Yahweh shalom -- The Lord calms all our fears.

Further on, in the book of Ruth, she and others are greeted by Boaz with the words: *"The Lord be with you."* They respond *"The Lord bless you."* Later Ruth will marry the powerful Boaz and become one of the ancestors of Jesus.

Then in the second book of Chronicles we read these words: *"The Lord is with you when you are with him, and if you seek him he will be present to you;"* Notice here the suggestion that we must do our part in seeking God and acknowledging his presence.

In the gospel of Luke the angel Gabriel comes to Mary and announces *"Hail, favored one! The Lord is with you."*

During the gathering for Mass two other forms for this greeting might be used by the Priest: *"The grace of our Lord Jesus Christ, and the love of God, and the communion of the Holy Spirit be with you all."*

The other form is: *"Grace to you and peace from God our Father and the Lord Jesus Christ."*

These greetings which include both the words "peace" and "grace" can be read in many of St. Paul's letters, such as Romans 1:7I,1 Corinthians 1:3, 2 Corinthians 13:13, Galatians 6:18, Philippians 4:23, as well as in 2 Timothy 4:22a, and Philemon 25.

"Peace" was the favored word of the Hebrews, while *"grace"* was the favored word of the Greeks. St. Paul often used both those words of greeting to early Christians who were both Hebrews and Greeks. So when we use Paul's greeting we too are embracing both our Hebrew and Gentile beginnings as Christians. This adds the suggestion that when the Priest and People enter into this dialogue of greeting with these words we're embracing all our ancestors in faith for thousands of years in recognizing that the grace of God is with us and brings us peace.

This greeting of peace is meant to say that the small and large current concerns of our lives are in the hands of God. We on our part must let them go in order to focus on God's presence and our belief that all will be well -- with God in our midst. So as the Priest holds out his hands in gracious welcome and assurance, the words he speaks are telling us to let go of the daily concerns because God is present with us. We can now peacefully begin to enter into the spiritual realm of God. As we answer, *"And with your spirit,"* we're saying to the Priest that we believe God is present in him as he takes on the role of Christ for us. Now we're all ready to pray the Mass together.

7. *In this next part as we're saying we're sorry why do our words seem to be saying a great deal more than that?*

The Penitential Act

JUST this title itself sounds pretty serious. What all is involved in this part of the Mass? The Penitential Act is simply an action of acknowledging ourselves as penitents, sinners. This action follows the Greeting and comes before the Gloria. It is perfectly positioned between our recognition of God's presence and our great prayer of praise to God which will come next. It's as if we're suddenly aware not only of God's presence but of the full grandeur of God Almighty. In this awareness we come to face our humanness in all our failings as well as the magnificent mercy of God who is always ready to forgive us.

The Priest begins with the following invitation:

"Brothers and sisters, let us acknowledge our sins and so prepare ourselves to celebrate the sacred mysteries."

After a brief pause for silent reflection, one of the following forms is used:

Priest and People all say this together:

I confess to almighty God
and to you, my brothers and sisters,
that I have greatly sinned,
in my thoughts and in my words,
in what I have done and
in what I have failed to do,
through my fault, through my fault,
through my most grievous fault;
therefore I ask blessed Mary ever-Virgin,
all the Angels and Saints,
and you, my brothers and sisters,
to pray for me to the Lord our God.

The Priest concludes with:

May almighty God have mercy on us,

> *forgive us our sins,*
> *and bring us to everlasting life.*

People*: Amen.*

The words of this prayer known as *the Confiteor* are quite amazing. The Priest and the People together are asking for forgiveness from God *and from each other*, all of us gathered at this moment. And then along with our brothers and sisters we ask Mary, our Mother, as well as the Angels and Saints to pray for us.

This reminds us that as we gather to pray as a Church, those who gather are not only those we can see with our eyes. We are also joined by all the Church including those down through the centuries who are now in Heaven. Finally, it is important for us to notice that as each of us asks for forgiveness our brothers and sisters are asking the same from us too.

Did you ever consider that we're saying *"I'm a sinner. I've done wrong. Please forgive me"* to our fellow parishioners right there beside us? And they are asking for our forgiveness. Pretty open and honest and powerful! Just consider that for a moment.

The second form sometimes used is a dialogue prayer between Priest and People:

Priest:	*Have mercy on us, O Lord.*
People:	*For we have sinned against you.*
Priest:	*Show us, O Lord, your mercy.*
People:	*And grant us your salvation.*
Priest:	*May almighty God have mercy on us,*
	forgive us our sins,
	and bring us to everlasting life.
People:	*Amen.*

After these first two forms the following petitions are requested in either English or Greek:

| Priest: | *Lord have mercy (or Kyrie, eleison)* |
| People: | *Lord have mercy (or Kyrie, eleison)* |

Priest:	*Christ have mercy (or Christe, eleison)*
People:	*Christ have mercy (or Christe, eleison)*
Priest:	*Lord have mercy (or Kyrie, eleison)*
People:	*Lord have mercy (or Kyrie, eleison)*

In a third form the Priest or Deacon makes the following type of prayer-petitions:

Priest:	*You were sent to heal the contrite of heart:*
	Lord have mercy (or Kyrie, eleison)
People:	*Lord have mercy (or Kyrie, eleison)*
Priest:	*You came to call sinners:*
	Christ have mercy (or Christe, eleison)
People:	*Christ have mercy (or Christe, eleison)*
Priest:	*You are seated at the right hand of the Father*
	to intercede for us:
	Lord have mercy (or Kyrie, eleison)
People:	*Lord have mercy (or Kyrie, eleison)*

(Lastly, regardless of which form is used, the Priest offers to God our prayer for forgiveness.)

Priest:	*May almighty God have mercy on us,*
	forgive us our sins,
	and bring us to everlasting life.
People:	*Amen.*

This is why our words are saying such a great deal more than it appears to us at first glance. During this Penitential Act of the Introductory Rite we're doing two very important things: we're making a communal admission of our sinfulness to God and to the whole community while also celebrating the amazing gift of God's great, unending mercy.

8. *Why are we suddenly shouting joyfully?*

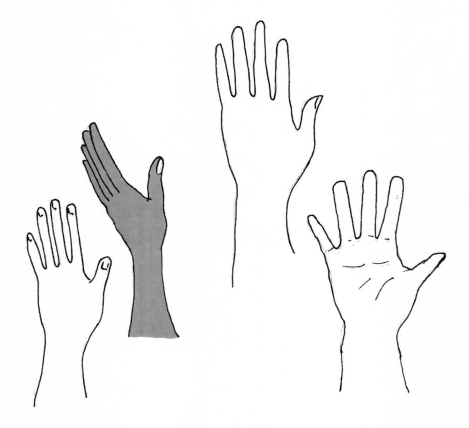

AEK

THE GLORIA

CONFIDENT that God in all his mercy will forgive our sins, we now turn our attention to the grandeur of God. We begin by joyfully praising God in the words from the Gospel of Luke which told of the angels who praised God at the birth of Jesus.

> *Glory to God in the highest,*
> *And on earth peace to people of good will.*

This prayer of the Gloria is an ancient hymn first recorded as being in use in 400 AD/CE. Following the song of the angels we continue to praise God with a variety of phrases. We're trying to express God's greatness in all the words we can use.

> *We praise you, we bless you, we adore you, we glorify you,*
> *we give you thanks for your great glory,*
> *Lord God, heavenly King, O God, almighty Father.*

Then we address Jesus in various titles and once again ask him to take away our sins.

> *Lord Jesus Christ, Only Begotten Son,*
> *Lord God, Lamb of God, Son of the Father*
> *you take away the sins of the world,*
> *   have mercy on us;*
> *you take away the sins of the world,*
> *   receive our prayer;*
> *you are seated at the right hand of the Father;*
> *   have mercy on us.*

In closing we give honor and praise to the Trinity: Father, Son and Holy Spirit.

> *For you alone are the Holy One,*
> *you alone are the Lord,*
> *you alone are the Most High,*
> *Jesus Christ,*

with the Holy Spirit,
In the glory of God the Father. Amen.

The best way to pray the Gloria is to sing it, adding to the joy of God's presence in our lives. It is a proclamation we're making to put God first in every moment of our lives. The Gloria is not included in Mass during Advent or Lent and some of our other Solemnities and Feasts. The reason for this is that during Advent we are "awaiting the coming" of the Lord at Christmas, and for the Second Coming at the end of time, as well as his coming into our hearts in a new way. During Lent we are focusing on what our lives would be like if Jesus had not come to save us. At the end of both Advent and Lent there's great joy in once again singing this very special and ancient prayer: The Gloria.

9. *They say if we listen closely we can hear four parts in this next prayer.*

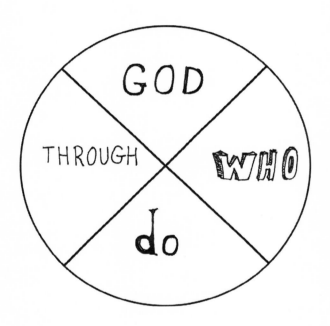

AEK

THE AMAZING COLLECT

THE Opening Prayer is also known as the Collect. The first thing to know about this word Collect is that it is pronounced: (COL' lect) with the emphasis on the first syllable. It looks like our familiar word "collect" and makes people think of the collection but it has nothing to do with that. The alternate term of Opening Prayer may also be confusing since there seems to have been prayers already said. This, however, is the first prayer said by the Presider and it is the Priest's way of setting the theme before us.

In the days of early Christianity the people who gathered would say out loud what they wished to ask of God. Now we consider our intentions silently. This prayer begins with the Priest saying: *"Let us pray."* To pray is to ask, so the Priest's words mean, let us ask God for help with our needs.

When the Priest says, *"Let us pray"* he then waits a few moments in silence. Often this silence is misinterpreted as if the Priest may have forgotten what he wants to say next or that the altar server has not yet arrived with the book. Many of us are busy at this time watching the altar server struggle to get over to the Priest with the book. Because of these incorrect assumptions we might miss the real purpose of *"Let us pray"* as we watch the movement in the sanctuary. This is what is really intended. The Priest says: *"Let us pray"* and waits in silence while we consider what our needs are for which we want to ask God's help. Then the Priest reads The Collect for that particular Mass. It's meant to be a *collection* of our needs especially as they relate to the day's theme or the liturgical season.

The Collect, almost always addressed to God the Father, is modeled after an ancient pattern of prayer. It's one sentence with four distinct parts. (God...Who...Do...Through)

1. God is addressed using one of the titles such as:

   "God Almighty ever-loving Father"

2. Then we remember and mention something God has done for us in the past which relates especially to the title we've just used (Father):

   "*who, sent Jesus to live with us as our brother*

3. Next we ask for something similar in the present: "

   bring to our hearts the spirit of adoption as your sons and daughters"

4. This prayer concludes with the doxology, the prayer of praise, naming through whom we are praying:

   "*through our Lord Jesus Christ, your Son, who lives and reigns with you in the unity of the Holy Spirit, one God, forever and ever.*"
   And the Assembly agrees with the prayer by answering:
   Amen."

It's an unusual construction and on first hearing it's hard to understand. If you listen closely though you'll begin to hear the lovely pattern by which we honor God's faithfulness in our lives and then ask God for similar help. It is with great awe toward God that we beg for our needs. With this posture of prayer we're now ready to hear from God.

10. HAPPY NEW YEAR ---
But why now?

OUR CATHOLIC LITURGICAL CALENDAR

HAPPY New Year seems like a greeting we save for January 1st. Yet, our Catholic year actually begins with the First Sunday of Advent which is celebrated either the last weekend of November or the first weekend of December. As far back as the history of human record we read that all people took note of the changing of the seasons. It was a way to explain the alterations of nature and also help mark the planting and harvesting times.

The Catholic Liturgical calendar is a way that the Church invites us to take note of how God's time breaks into our lives. It offers us a way to focus on the spiritual dimension of our lives and relate this to our familiar seasons of nature.

The Catholic Liturgical year begins with the celebration of God coming into our world to be with us. In the course of the year we'll hear the story of God-with-us in many ways: both in the covenant made with our Hebrew ancestors and the second covenant that Jesus made through his life, death and resurrection.

A brief overview of The Catholic Liturgical Year shows that the year is divided into two major cycles. The first cycle begins near the end of our calendar year with the spiritual preparation of Advent and continues through Christmas Time. During Advent we prepare for the coming of Jesus into our world. Then throughout Christmas Time we celebrate Jesus' birth and some key early life events.

This is followed in January and a bit beyond that by the first series of Ordinary Time when week by week we hear the story unfold of Jesus' life.

The second major cycle begins on Ash Wednesday with the spiritual preparation of Lent. This will continue through six weeks and end as Easter Time begins. The most important time of the whole Liturgical Year comes on the feast of Easter when we celebrate the Resurrection of Jesus from the dead. This is the awesome miraculous, mysterious moment on which all of the Christian faith rests

Easter Time continues throughout 50 days until Pentecost when we celebrate the Holy Spirit pouring out on us the strength to continue God's work. At this point on the calendar we enter the second series of Ordinary Time during which we learn about the beginnings of the early Church, how we are to "be church" in the world and how to prepare ourselves for eternal life.

There is a Section at the end of this book which will describe each part of the Catholic Liturgical Year in more detail. When you read those pages and see how these various Times unfold it will help in understanding why certain readings are chosen for each Mass and how each weekly liturgy has a theme that fits the particular Time.

11. *Why do we always read from the Bible?*

AEK

The Liturgy of the Word

THINK of all the times when we sit around with each other and tell stories about amazing events we've witnessed or experienced of even just heard about from others. We all want to know the actual details of an amazing happening. We want to relive the event through these stories. In the same way at early Christian gatherings it was customary for them to read accounts from the Apostles and disciples about all that had happened when they encountered Jesus.

Also, when we think of the earliest Christians, remember most of them were fervent Jews. What they were used to in their worship services is having the High Priest or a Rabbi read from the Scriptures. We know that Jesus read from the Scriptures in the synagogue. This was a normal occurrence for our Hebrew ancestors—a way to connect with God and remind them of God's covenant and their promises to God. For the earliest Christians this would seem normal for them to read about God, to read what God said to them and to ponder what their part in all this should be.

That is a description of the ancient worship service which has the same familiar pattern we experience today in our Liturgy of the Word. Several selections from Sacred Scripture are read and sung followed by the priest's homily.

In the Sunday Liturgy of the Word we have

> The First Reading
> followed by The Responsorial Psalm
> The Second Reading
> The Gospel Acclamation introducing
> The Gospel
> The Homily
> The Creed
> The Prayer of the Faithful

When the phrase "word of God" is used this can mean the Scriptures from the Holy Bible or it can mean Jesus, the incarnate Word of God, as Jesus is referred to in the first chapter of the Gospel of John. Jesus, the Word of God, entered into our human world and walked the same earth we travel. In a different way but just as true for us, God is always alive in the world he is creating and this is what we hear when we listen to the Scripture readings. We witness God entering our human events and hearts, we hear God speaking to people and see him working in their lives. We experience God relating consistently and continuously through a mutual covenant of faithfulness and love.

In the Vatican Council II document entitled *Sacrosanctum Concilium - The Constitution on Sacred Liturgy* #7 [21] we read: (Christ) "is present in the Word, since it is he himself who speaks when the holy Scriptures are read in the Church." Jesus Christ comes to nourish us in the Liturgy of the Word just as we know he comes to offer himself to us as nourishment in the Liturgy of the Eucharist.

Up to this point in the Mass the Assembly has been standing. This is a posture of prayer that was customary for our Jewish ancestors. It signifies that we're actively attending to what is occurring, we're ready to take part, we're showing respect and giving praise. After the Priest prays the Collect, the Assembly will sit. This shows we're ready to listen and be receptive to what we hear. We're going to listen to the story of God's constant action in our human history. The Sacred Scriptures are God's self-communication, God's self-revelation to us. The readings are in the chronological order of our salvation history.

Since Vatican Council II the Sunday Scriptures are organized in three-year cycles beginning each year on the First Sunday of Advent.

Throughout Year A the Gospel of Matthew is read.

During Year B we read the Gospel of Mark,

and in Year C we'll hear the Gospel of Luke.

The fourth book, the Gospel of John is sometimes referred to as "high Christology" which signifies it is written to emphasize the Godly Divinity of Jesus. This Gospel book is not given a separate cycle, a separate year, but is used in special places particularly during Advent, Lent and Easter Time and to fill out the shorter Gospel of Mark in Year B.

Prior to the use of this three year cycle most Gospel choices were from Matthew only. Now we hear from the entire four Gospels in the course of three years. The Book of Gospels is a sacred book containing the Gospel Readings for Sunday Masses and other Solemnities of the Church calendar, such as Christmas. This is the book that is carried in the Entrance procession and placed on the altar at the beginning of Mass.

The Gospel is read last but has been chosen first, according to the season and feast.

The First Reading taken from the Old Testament, is chosen to complement the Gospel. This pairing is based on various reasons:

> to show a foreshadowing from the Hebrew Scriptures (the Old Testament) of something that later will be heard in the Gospel taken from the Christian Scriptures (the New Testament);
> and if the Gospel reading quotes from an Old Testament passage that same Old Testament reading may be chosen to show continuity between Old & New.

Before Vatican Council II few of the Old Testament Scriptures were read and now you can experience selections from almost all the Old Testament books.

The Responsorial Psalm is chosen in most cases as an appropriate response to the First Reading. Or, if the Gospel of the day quotes from a certain Psalm often that same Psalm will be used. Certain particular feasts have long since been associated with a special Psalm and that also is still used as a guideline of choice. There are 150 Psalms. Today 80 of them are read on Sundays and 40 others are read on the weekdays. 130 psalms altogether are read in the course of a year.

The Second Reading, read on Sundays but not read on the weekdays, is chosen from the epistles, a word that means "letters." The 21 letters in the New Testament were written mainly by St. Paul and other Christian leaders to the newly growing Christian communities. This reading is not chosen to complement the others. Rather, for a series of days or weeks, one epistle at a time is read from beginning to end mainly to acquaint the people with the early church and with the initial directives on how to live a Christian life. During Advent, Christmas Time, Lent and Easter Time certain epistle selections are chosen to make a purposeful connection with the other readings. The Lectionary is a sacred book containing the Scripture Readings organized for each day's proclamation. We now read part or all of most of the epistles.

The Gospel Acclamation is a very short Scripture selection.

This Scriptural quotation is most often sung with "Alleluia" coming before and after it. This selection is usually taken from one line within the Gospel that will be read. This is a way to graciously and prayerfully take notice that we're about to hear the words of Jesus.

Again, the order in which all these readings are set in the Mass is as follows:

> The First Reading followed by The Responsorial Psalm
> The Second Reading
> The Gospel Acclamation introducing The Gospel

There are a few more thoughts in the following pages of this book about each of these Readings to give you a fuller idea of why each one is important to be read and what each might have to offer us.

It's enriching for us to read and pray over the readings both before and after Mass. References to locate the readings can be found in parish bulletins, on parish websites and at www.USCCB.org. As we hear the Scripture readings proclaimed at every Mass, it's important for us to develop within ourselves the same sense of awe for the word of God that the Hebrew people had. As you listen, don't be concerned about remembering everything but rather pray to hear and remember one word of inspiration that God knows you alone need right now in your life. Our lives can take on new meaning when the word of God is heard.

12. What parts of the Bible are used for the First Reading? Why these parts?

THE FIRST READING

IT seems to make some sense when telling a story that we start at the beginning. Our faith history as it is recorded starts with the first books in the Bible. That's why <u>The First Reading</u> is taken from the Hebrew Scriptures (Old Testament) and sometimes from the books of *Acts* or *Revelation* in the Christian Scriptures (New Testament). In the First Reading we hear the Israelites' history of their relationship with God. We hear them tell of creation; of Abraham's covenant of faith with God and his journey to Canaan. We hear about their Exodus from Egypt and the years of wandering in the desert leading to the Promised Land. We hear about the promise of a messiah to come in the future. Throughout all these recollections of human spiritual history what we hear is that the people are sometimes faithful to their covenant with God and their spiritual practices yet often unfaithful. From God we always, always hear faithfulness to his people. Later when the Priest offers the Homily to help us make good spiritual use of the Readings we may understand more clearly how these stories from ancient times are not only about the old days but about today, about our individual lives and the spiritual journey we're each traveling.

The responses at the end of the Reading show respect for our Hebrew and early Christian ancestors. Our Hebrew ancestors avoided saying the name of God out of respect and awe. Instead they chose to use the Hebrew equivalent of "Lord" and the lector follows their example in this.

At the end of the First Reading the Lector says:
"The Word of the Lord."

The Assembly responds:
"Thanks be to God."

This second response common to the ancient people appears in many of St. Paul's epistles. We're saying that we're grateful for God's word which has nourished our spirit to help us better live a Christ-filled life. In listening later to the Gospel, notice that this First Reading has been chosen purposely to reflect the Gospel selection.

13. *I have no idea what's going on in this part or what I'm supposed to do. It sounds like the children's game of Marco Polo.*

THE RESPONSORIAL PSALM

MY friend, the young mother with two little ones, said that this part sounded to her like the children's game of Marco Polo. Actually her comment is right on target. In that game all the players hide while one person shouts out "Marco" and the others echo their answer "Polo". The object of the game is to find each other and connect with one another. Connecting is what this prayer is all about. The Assembly is connecting with the cantor, together we're connecting with our Hebrew ancestors, and we're all connecting with God in this response to the word of God we've just heard in the First Reading.

The Responsorial Psalm is the second part of the Liturgy of the Word. We all sing or say this together. The cantor will sing the verses from the Book of Psalms and the Assembly will respond. That's the meaning of the name given to this part. It's the style for singing or praying in two parts the lovely prayers, poems and songs taken mostly from the Book of Psalms.

This Scriptural selection is not just meant to be an interlude between the other two readings. It reflects the First Reading and has an importance of its own. This is the portion of the Old Testament (Hebrew Scriptures) that the Hebrew people used for prayer and song in their worship. These Psalms express many different emotions such as praise, joy, gratitude, trust, awe and wonder, dejection, anger, lament, hopelessness, thanksgiving, as well as requests for forgiveness, guidance, compassion, protection, rescue, justice and mercy. As you read the Psalms you can actually imagine real people in open and honest exchange with God. These songs and prayers are as alive as our conversations today. The Psalm chosen for each liturgy will connect with the emotional tone of the First Reading. It is intended as a response from the People to the words just spoken by or about God. It makes a connection. In some form or other this Hebrew tradition of praying or singing the Psalms was continued in the early church by the first Hebrew Christians and later by the Desert Fathers & Mothers. In later centuries when monasteries first formed the monks developed a pattern for singing or praying the Psalms throughout the day and night. The Psalms are the basis for what's known today as the Liturgy of the Hours, considered "the Prayer of the Church."

Most faithful Jewish people of ancient times knew the 150 psalms by heart. Imagine Jesus himself, as a young boy and later as a young man, knew by heart and prayed these very same verses we pray today. It's said that Jesus quoted the Psalms more than any other book of Scripture. Just think about these quotes from Jesus' last words:

> My god, my God, why have you abandoned me. Psalm 22:2a
> Into your hands I commend my spirit. Psalm 31:6a

It can be very spiritually enlightening to read those psalms in full to understand what Jesus might have meant by those few words. As we sing or recite the Responsorial Psalm, we're praying with Jesus and all our spiritual ancestors. And if we can let even one phrase or one word enter our memory we'll have spiritual nourishment for the whole week.

14. Is this reading from the Bible too?

IMAGINE trying to tell people all about Jesus, his life, his teachings, that he died and then rose from the dead and that he was the Son of God! People might say: nice thoughts but an unbelievably tall story at best. Yet this is what the Epistles do.

The Second Reading is drawn from the Epistles, letters which contained the earliest writings of the Christian Scriptures (New Testament). In many different cities from Jerusalem to Rome and far beyond, the apostles and other disciples were going forth to tell this story. In all those places small groups of people began to form Christian communities dedicated to Jesus Christ and his message. These early church groups needed and wanted to hear more about Jesus: his life, death, resurrection, his teachings and the mission to build the kingdom of God on earth. They needed guidance, direction and courage. So, St. Paul, other apostles and disciples, most of whom were eye witnesses to Jesus' life on earth, began to write letters (epistles) to these small developing communities. Even though the Epistles, (letters) are found at the end of the New Testament (Christian Scriptures) following the Gospels, they actually were written before the Gospels. After we hear in the First Reading about the Hebrew story, these Epistles represent the next chronological chapter in our recorded Christian family history. That's why they are placed as the Second Reading of the Mass.

The early Church Communities would gather, often in their homes, and read these Epistles together. In this way these early believers learned that Christ was indeed the fulfillment of all faith history—the Messiah. They learned that Jesus Christ IS the New Covenant, the Son of God. The believers were being called to share in Christ's Passion, Death and the victory of his Resurrection. Those who wrote the Epistles were trying to help the new believers absorb what this meant for them in living their lives. In other words, these writings represented the inspired authors' guidance on how to be disciples of Christ each and every day.

In those early times both the writers and those who read the Epistles were often called The People of the Way to signify they were on a journey of spiritual growth. The Epistles served as their guide. This is the same purpose they provide today, a guide for us on our way. In the days when these first Epistle authors wrote, spreading the message by word and example, everyone depended on them. Now it all depends on us.

Just as with the First Reading, at the end of the Second Reading, the Lector says:

"The Word of the Lord."
And the Assembly responds:
"Thanks be to God."

15. Why is there a procession and singing before the next reading?

AEK

THE GOSPEL ACCLAMATION

THIS time we're not going to hear about Jesus but the actual words of Jesus. This is big! To respond to this the People stand to show they are actively participating and showing the greatest respect for the actual word of God. The Acclamation itself consists of praying or singing the "Alleluia" along with a single phrase quoting from the Gospel passage which is about to be read. The Gospel Acclamation is meant to show great joyful expectation and praise for Jesus Christ whose word we are about to hear proclaimed by the Priest or Deacon.

During this singing, if the Deacon is going to proclaim the Gospel, he bows profoundly before the Priest, asking for the blessing, saying in a low voice: "Your blessing, Father."

The Priest blesses the Deacon while he says in a low voice:

> "May the Lord be in your heart and on your lips, that you may proclaim his Gospel worthily and well, in the name of the Father, and of the Son, + and of the Holy Spirit."

The Deacon signs himself with the Sign of the Cross and replies: "Amen."

If the Priest is going to be the one to proclaim the Gospel, he bows before the altar, and says quietly:

> "Cleanse my heart and my lips, almighty God, that I may worthily proclaim your holy Gospel."

The Book of Gospels which was placed at the center of the altar at the beginning of the Mass is now taken by the Priest from the altar, in the second procession of the Mass, to the ambo, the place from where the Gospel will be read. The Book of the Gospels is held high, we the People are standing and singing, all to give great honor to Jesus Christ. This is the grandest moment in the Liturgy of the Word. In the earlier Readings we heard *about* Jesus. Now we're going to hear *from* Jesus. The Assembly is gratefully celebrating that the Risen Lord is in our midst about to speak to us and we are ready to listen.

Jesus Christ will be speaking to his assembled Church through the inspired writings of the Gospels. This is a good moment to realize that Jesus is speaking this same message at every Mass in every country throughout the whole world. Amazing!

16. Another Bible reading?
    What's special about this one?

THE GOSPEL

PICTURE yourself sitting on a hillside in Galilee with folks from towns all around. You can hear the gentle waves from the Sea of Galilee, feel the breezes in the surrounding brush and see the outline of the hillside across the waters. All this while you are hearing the challenging message of love from the Son of God himself. That's what's special about this Reading.

Before the Gospel is proclaimed the Deacon or Priest addresses the Assembly: *"The Lord be with you."*
The Assembly stands and replies: *And with your spirit."*

Then the Deacon or the Priest announces:

> *"A reading from the holy Gospel according to (Matthew, Mark, Luke or John)."*

At the same time he makes the Sign of the Cross on the book and on his forehead, lips, and heart.

Just as the Priest blessed himself some of the People also do that as they quietly recite words similar to those said by the Priest:

> *"May the words of the Gospel be in my mind, on my lips and in my heart."*

This custom expresses people's desire to take the message of the good news into their whole beings in order to be transformed. When God's word enters our hearts it can change our lives.

The People respond to the announcement of the Gospel:

> *"Glory to you, O Lord."*

That response reminds us that we believe Jesus Christ is present in our midst and through the inspired words of the Gospel authors we're being nourished by God. The Gospel / the Good News is that God has come among us and the Spirit is with us still. We listen as one of the four Gospel accounts of Jesus' life and teachings sink into our thoughts and hearts. For a Christian, only from the perspective of the Gospel is the Old Testament text understood in its fullness. The Old Testament spoke consistently of a covenant between God and his people. In the New Testament we hear that Jesus IS the new covenant.

The Gospel reading is not meant as an occasion to just learn about God, nor is it just a story about our past spiritual history. The Gospel has a much deeper meaning for us today as we hear Jesus speak helping us to live our lives as good and loving Christians.

In describing the four gospels let's first imagine for an example that we were going to describe where we live to four different people. The first person lives in the same City as we do; the second person doesn't live in the same City but does live in the same State; the third person doesn't live in the same State at all but another State in our Country; and the fourth person lives in an entirely different Country. Because each of these four persons lives in a different area with different surroundings and maybe even different cultures we would have to create four separate descriptions that would make sense to each of these four people. Why? Because they each have a vantage point distinct from the others.

This is the way it was with the writing of the four gospels. Each of the four Gospels offers us a different style. This was most likely because they were written for different groups of people with varying life circumstances. Here's a brief summary of the four. The Gospel of Mark which Scripture scholars today seem to believe was the first to be written was probably intended for Christians facing persecution and possibly even death. Mark was likely the person who traveled with Peter and at other times with Paul.

Mark knew firsthand the steep price for people at that time just to be Christian. Mark's Gospel describes Jesus and his mission as one of intense suffering and sacrifice. Jesus thought to be the royal messiah was indeed a king. But Mark's version of this king is one of a suffering servant whose mission is to serve.

In Matthew's Gospel we see a deliberate and continual showing of Jesus' life and death as the fulfillment of the Torah the first five books of the Old Testament which recorded their creation, their covenant with God, the promise of a messiah and the Law handed down to them from God through Moses. This Gospel of Matthew is written in a particular style for people of his day who knew their Scriptures well. Most likely Matthew was writing for the early Christians who were primarily practicing Jews and had been waiting for the promised messiah.

Luke's Gospel is emotional, passionate and interpersonal with a focus on individuals and personal relationships. This is the gospel that features the stories of the Prodigal Son, the Good Samaritan, the call of Zachaeus and the dramatic and poignant description of the Good Thief. Many women are featured in Luke's accounts and there is a strong focus on Jesus' mother Mary. Luke's primary readers were perhaps not all Jews but rather many who were the early Greek Christians. They would not be in need of Old Testament fulfillment stories and would be more open to the interpersonal relationships of Jesus.

John's Gospel is not one of the three "synoptic" Gospels meaning the three other Gospels that told Jesus' story with a similar historical timeline. John's Gospel was written several decades later when the message of Christianity had been spread already to quite a great number of people. John's Gospel seems to be stating very strongly that Jesus is truly God Incarnate. John's rendering of Jesus and his teachings is more majestic, poetic, symbolic and philosophic. It begins with these words: "In the beginning was the Word, and the Word was with God and the Word was God." The divinity of Jesus is stressed from start to finish.

Whether the Gospel Reading is from Matthew, Mark, Luke or John, we the People listen with an open heart so that the message of Jesus' words can touch, heal and transform us. The Readings feed us, nourish us in order to form us ever more deeply as People of God today.

At the end the Deacon or Priest acclaims: *"The Gospel of the Lord."*

We reply: *"Praise to you, Lord Jesus Christ."* Then the Priest kisses the book, saying quietly: *"Through the words of the Gospel may our sins be wiped away."* After listening to the Gospel, the People will be seated, in a receptive posture, to listen to the Homily.

17. *Why is there a sudden break in the procedure and the priest acts so differently, talking directly to the people?*

THE HOMILY

THERE is a wonderful Gospel story you may know which is referred to as The Road to Emmaus. (Luke 24:13-35) In this story we read about some followers of Jesus who became distraught when they found that the tomb where Jesus' body had been laid was now empty. They met a man there on the road who seemed not to know about anything that had just happened in Jerusalem. They told him about Jesus' suffering and death and now his disappearance. The "stranger" then "opened their minds to understand the scriptures." Later when they broke bread together they recognized that the "stranger" was Jesus and they said to themselves "Were not our hearts burning within us while he spoke to us on the way and opened the scriptures to us?"

This is what happens in the homily. While the People sit in a receptive posture, the Priest (in the person of Christ) opens the meaning of the Scripture readings for the People to understand more fully how the word of God is speaking to us now and relates to our lives today. That's why the Priest seems more natural. He's talking about this day in our current lives and his life too. The Priest breaks open the word to offer us nourishment, strengthening us in our Christian lives. God is always entering our human history continually offering us hope, challenging us to grow in love, and grounding us in our faith. The Priest applies the message for the day to our current situations so that we might bring the word of God into the reality of our daily lives.

We've come together as a family to praise God and to be encouraged to live a Christian life in our world today. Sometimes Jesus' words and the homily that explains it comfort the afflicted among us and other times they afflict the comfortable parts of our lives, challenging us to grow. Sometimes we are warmed by the message of God's faithful love and at other times we are troubled by the challenge it presents.

We're like the disciples on the road to Emmaus who felt their hearts were burning with the message of Jesus, both with joy and trepidation. They were comforted later when they recognized Jesus in the breaking of the bread. That's also what will happen for us soon as the Mass progresses.

Before Vatican Council II this part of the Mass used to be called the sermon in which the Priest would lecture to the Assembly about any topic. Today this is called the homily in which the Priest interprets and applies the Scriptures to help nourish the People. The People should pray for the homilist so that through his words we'll be moved to a deeper relationship with God.

It's at this point in the Mass that the Catechumens, those studying and preparing for Baptism, will be dismissed to continue their preparation. This was a custom from the earliest days of the first Christian communities. It's now been revived.

18. Why do we stand now?
What's different here?

THE CREED

THE People now stand to pray the Creed. When we stand we come out of our reflective listening posture and are together again in an active prayer posture. We're involved with all those in attendance with us and consciously paying attention with respect to what we're about to do.

We've just heard the word of God and now we're going to respond by praying to God about what we believe. Together we say "I believe..." as we state the essential beliefs we hold as Catholic Christians. We profess together what we believe as it's been revealed to all of us and to the whole world by God through the Sacred Scriptures. This is a rededication to our original Baptismal promises. When a Baptism is celebrated during Mass or at the Easter Vigil we too renew our Baptismal promises instead of saying the Creed.

The Apostles Creed was used for Baptism in the days of the early Church. While this is sometimes said, the more common creed that is used today is the Nicene Creed. The first origins of this Creed come from the Council of Nicaea in the 4th century. The Creed itself seems to have been first used in the 6th century and then became the official form in the 11th century. This prayer is commonly referred to as The Creed since *credo* is the Latin word for "I believe."

The essential beliefs we state in this prayer will focus on the Trinity – the Father, the Son and the Holy Spirit. The prayer begins with stating "I believe in one God, the Father Almighty." Then the largest part of the prayer is focused on Jesus, the Son of God, about his coming into the human world, living among us, suffering, dying, and rising from the dead. Then the words of the Creed profess belief in the Holy Spirit. Finally there's a short listing of beliefs at the end which refer to the Church, Baptism and to eternal life. *The Catechism of the Catholic Church* has a very clear and extensive explanation about each element in this prayer.

> I believe in one God,
> the Father almighty,

maker of heaven and earth,
of all things visible and invisible.

I believe in one Lord Jesus Christ,
the Only Begotten Son of God,
born of the Father before all ages.
God from God, Light from Light,
true God from true God,
begotten, not made, consubstantial with the Father;
through him all things were made.
For us men and for our salvation
he came down from heaven,
and by the Holy Spirit was incarnate of the Virgin Mary,
and became man.
For our sake he was crucified under Pontius Pilate,
he suffered death and was buried,
and rose again on the third day
in accordance with the Scriptures.
He ascended into heaven
and is seated at the right hand of the Father.
He will come again in glory
to judge the living and the dead
and his kingdom will have no end.

I believe in the Holy Spirit, the Lord, the giver of life,
who proceeds from the Father and the Son,
who with the Father and the Son is adored and glorified,
who has spoken through the prophets.

I believe in one, holy, catholic and apostolic Church.
I confess one Baptism for the forgiveness of sins
and I look forward to the resurrection of the dead
and the life of the world to come. Amen.

19. Why do we make all these specific prayer requests?

THE UNIVERSAL PRAYER / THE PRAYER OF THE FAITHFUL

DID you know that as baptized persons we have been anointed to be priest, prophet and king? Yes, it's true. As unordained priests we have the responsibility to hold up the world to God in prayer making all things holy. In the role of prophet we must speak God's truth in our words and our actions. And as king we are to protect and nurture those in need, as a benevolent ruler would do for the people. Those not yet baptized are called Catechumens and those who are baptized are called the Faithful which is why one of the names for this prayer is The Prayer of the Faithful, those baptized.

In our anointed role as a priestly people we should pray for everyone in the whole world and that's why this part of the Mass is also called The Universal Prayer. It's at this time when we leave our own concerns behind and bring the cares and needs of others to mind in prayer. This prayer broadens our vision and reminds us that we're part of a global community. We're among one billion Catholics in the world and we're also part of the life of every human being in the world.

It's suggested that we pray for

> the needs of the Church and it's leaders;
> public authorities & the salvation of the whole world;
> those burdened by any kind of difficulty or hardship;
> the needs of the local community, including the sick
> and those recently deceased in the parish.

While this format is suggested, the composition is left to the local parish and is often prepared by the Deacon week by week, according to the needs of both the local and the larger community. It's assumed that the Deacon who is ordained to minister to the community's needs will know best who is in need of prayers. While many parishes today have deacons serving, there are also many parishes who have no experience of a deacon. These duties are then part of the liturgical preparation team of a parish. It's the only prayer of the liturgy that is not written and prescribed for all to read the same words. It is written to relate to the concerns of the world and of those who will be in attendance at each particular liturgy.

The Prayer is first introduced by the Priest. The Lector, Deacon or Priest offers the individual petitions & then requests that we pray, with a phrase such as,

> "Let us pray to the Lord."

The actual prayer occurs when the Faithful respond, saying:

> "Lord hear our prayer."

At the end of all the petitions the Priest offers a concluding prayer. This Prayer of the Faithful is actually the first offering that the People make to God as we begin the next part of the liturgy with the offering of the other gifts.

20. Why does it feel like something has shifted at this point?

AEK

THE LITURGY OF THE EUCHARIST

DURING this part of the Mass, the Sacrifice of Jesus crucified for us is made present again in order for the People assembled to take part. At the Last Supper Jesus *took* bread and wine, *blessed* it, *broke* it and *shared* it with his Apostles saying: "Do this in remembrance of me." For the Hebrew people to remember is not just to recall but to make something come alive again in the present. This is what the Priest, in the person of Christ, is going to make happen. That's why it feels more serious now.

We who are assembled now prepare ourselves and the gifts to be offered for the Eucharistic sacrifice. The preparation will include:

-- the Presentation and Preparation of the Gifts, and

-- the Prayer over the Offerings.

During the <u>Presentation of the Gifts</u> the Priest and the People are all actively involved. A monetary collection is taken throughout the church. These funds will help pay for the actual material needs of maintaining the church as well as all the pastoral and educational needs of the People, especially those in great need. As the bread and wine is brought forth for consecration so too is this collection. All of these gifts represent the People offering ourselves to God. From the many gifts of God's creation, including our own lives, we now offer all of these back to God as our gift in return.

At this time we experience the third procession. Just as the gifts to be offered represent the lives of those assembled, a few parishioners will represent all those in attendance. In the name of all they will bring the gifts in procession from the back of the church up the aisle to be accepted by the priest before the altar. By way of joining in this third procession the People sing an offering of ourselves. We are journeying together toward the altar to offer our gifts which represent ourselves.

While the collection and procession are taking place the altar is prepared for the reception of the gifts. The altar servers place on the altar the linens, the Missal and the sacred vessels. When the procession reaches the sanctuary the Priest accepts the gifts and places them on the altar. Or we might say we symbolically are placed in the hands of God, which is what the altar represents. These actions begin what is called the <u>Preparation of the Gifts</u>.

The following prayers are said silently or sometimes out loud, first over the bread and then over the wine with a response each time from the People.

Priest: Blessed are you, Lord God of all creation, for through your goodness we have received the bread we offer you: fruit of the earth and work of human hands, it will become for us the bread of life.

People: Blessed be God for ever.

Priest: (The Priest pours wine and a little water into the chalice, praying silently.)
By the mystery of this water and wine may we come to share in the divinity of Christ who humbles himself to share in our humanity.

Priest: Blessed are you, Lord God of all creation, for through your goodness we have received the wine we offer you: fruit of the vine and work of human hands. It will become our spiritual drink.

People: Blessed be God forever.

(Priest praying silently):

With humble spirit and contrite heart may we be accepted by you, O Lord, and may our sacrifice in your sight this day be pleasing to you, Lord God.

Finally, the Priest washes his hands. Originally this was a necessity since the gifts offered in earlier days were livestock or harvest from the fields. Today this same action serves as a symbol of interior cleansing in preparation for what is to come next.

(Priest praying silently):

Wash me, O Lord, from my iniquity and cleanse me from my sin.

Now there is a short meaningful dialogue as the Priest invites the People to pray that the gifts will be found acceptable by God.

Priest: Pray brothers and sisters, that my sacrifice and yours may be acceptable to God, the almighty Father.

People: May the Lord accept the sacrifice at your hands, for the praise and glory of his name, for our good, and the good of all his holy Church.

The Priest concludes this dialogue as he says the <u>Prayer over the Offerings</u> which will be different for each Mass reflecting the overall theme of the particular liturgy of the day.

The People give assent to this prayer by saying: Amen.

Now the preparation is complete. The Priest continues with the Liturgy of the Eucharist as he begins the Eucharistic Prayer.

21. Why is this part so long and quiet?
And how are we supposed to be
involved in it?

THE EUCHARISTIC PRAYER

NOW the liturgy moves into the Eucharistic Prayer which is perhaps the most solemn part of the entire Mass. The sense we have is that this is the longest prayer ever that the Priest says by himself. Actually, it is a series of short prayers with several acclamations given by the People. The Priest calls upon the People to lift up our hearts in prayer. He will be praying in the name of all the People and himself *to God the Father* through Jesus Christ in the Holy Spirit. We are praying together, the Priest in the person of Christ, to God our Father in thanksgiving and in the offering of sacrifice.

There are four main Eucharistic Prayers, each with a different theme. There are nine others used for special occasions.

All versions of the Eucharistic Prayer will include the following parts:

The Preface	(Priest and People)
The Acclamation	(Priest and People)
The Epiclesis	(Priest to the Holy Spirit)
The Institution Narrative	(Priest in the person of Jesus Christ)
The Mystery of Faith	(Priest and People)
The Anamnesis	(Priest "remembers")
The Oblation	(Priest to God our Father for unity)
The Intercessions	(Priest)
The Concluding Doxology	(Priest)
The Great Amen	(People)

The Preface, a prayer during which the People stand to give glory, praise and thanks to God, includes three parts:

-- a Dialogue between the Priest and the People
-- the Priest prays the Preface
-- the People respond with an Acclamation

Priest: The Lord be with you
(Now the People will stand to be actively involved.)

People: And with your spirit.
Priest: Lift up your hearts.
People: We lift them up to the Lord.
Priest: Let us give thanks to the Lord, our God.
People: It is right and just.

The Priest continues to pray one of several possible choices of a Preface, chosen according to the overall theme of each particular Mass.

The Acclamation. When the Priest has finished the prayer the People acclaim his words with the beautiful, ancient prayer known as the Sanctus or the Holy, Holy.

All: Holy, holy, holy Lord God of hosts.
         Heaven and earth are full of your glory.
         Hosanna in the highest.
         Blessed is he who comes in the name of the Lord.
         Hosanna in the highest.

What we are trying to express in this Acclamation is that Glory is bursting forth all around us because God – right here, right now -- is coming into our lives.

To appreciate the ancient beauty and use of this prayer by our spiritual ancestors you can see here a listing of Scriptural references for our prayer "Sanctus" / "Holy, holy" which you might want to read. They all have the same intent we are trying to express.

Isaiah 6:3 "Holy, holy, holy is the Lord of hosts!" they cried one to the other. "All the earth is filled with his glory!" At the sound of that cry, the frame of the door shook and the house was filled with smoke.

Psalm 118:26 Blessed is he who comes in the name of the Lord.

Matthew 21:9 The crowds preceding him and those following kept crying out and saying: "Hosanna to the Son of David; blessed is he who comes in the name of the Lord; hosanna in the highest."

Mark 11:9-10 Those preceding him as well as those following kept crying out: "Hosanna! Blessed is he who comes in the name of the Lord! Blessed is the kingdom of our father David that is to come! Hosanna in the highest!"

Revelation 4:8 The four living creatures, each of them with six wings, were covered with eyes inside and out. Day and night they do not stop exclaiming: "Holy, holy, holy is the Lord God almighty, who was, and who is, and who is to come."

At the end of praying the "Sanctus/Holy, Holy" the People all kneel. Now in this posture we're expressing our most humble, prayerful meditative gesture. As we kneel we tend to go inward and separate from others as we connect profoundly with God. You may notice the church atmosphere starts to become very still and quiet.

The next section of the Eucharistic Prayer is called *the Epiclesis (the invocation or calling down of the Holy Spirit)*. The Priest will call upon the Holy Spirit to make holy the gifts which we're offering.

This is followed by *the Institution Narrative,* also known as the Consecration of the bread and wine into the Body and Blood of Jesus Christ. This is the most solemn part of the Mass. You can tell that the People are aware of this since the whole church is now very quiet, almost as if no one is moving or even breathing, except perhaps a baby whose noise only serves to highlight the beauty of God.

The prayers said here by the Priest are taken from the Gospels as they are the remembered words of Jesus himself at the Last Supper:

Matt 26:26-28; Mk 14:22-26; Luke 22:14-23; 1 Corinthians 11:23-25

In all these references we read of four actions of Jesus. He *took* the bread and wine, *blessed* it, *broke* it and gave it to the Apostles to *share* in eating this meal together. *Take, bless, break, share* – these are the hallmarks of *the Institution Narrative.* They also provide many symbolic images of what happens on our spiritual journey of life.

After the consecration, the Priest announces to the People "*The Mystery of Faith.*" Again, the People are asked to acclaim our belief in what has just taken place. In the People's response we are saying: Yes, we too believe in this great mystery of our faith, that Jesus is now present with us in his Body and Blood. This is what is meant by "the Real Presence." The People express this in an act of faith with the words from one of three choices:

People: We proclaim your Death, O Lord,
and profess your Resurrection
until you come again.

or   When we eat this Bread and drink this Cup,
We proclaim your Death, O Lord,
until you come again.

or   Save us, Savior of the world, for by your Cross and
Resurrection you have set us free.

Next we come to the prayer know as *the Anamnesis* (the remembering). The Priest now makes a special point in remembering all that Jesus has done for us through his life, death and resurrection. Then the Priest offers the Body and Blood of Jesus to the Father asking that it be an acceptable sacrifice for salvation.

In *the Oblation or 2nd Epiclesis* the Priest calls on God to bring down unity among all those who will soon receive the Body and Blood of Christ.

Here will follow *the Intercessions* for the pope, the local bishop, all bishops, the clergy, the Church, for all gathered at this time and place, and for all people who sincerely seek God. Also included are those who have died and the hope we have that they have now joined Mary, Joseph, the Apostles and all the Saints in heaven.

The Concluding Doxology will bring this series of prayers to a close with the praise and glory of the Trinity -- Father, Son and Holy Spirit. The People again respond with strong and full belief for all that has been said by the Priest and taken place throughout the Eucharistic Prayer. Here the word *Amen* generally means "we the People are in full agreement with all that the Priest has said and done." This response given with full and strong emphasis by the People is called *the Great Amen*.

To emphasize the grand agreement of this Great Amen this response is often sung by the People. Holding up the Body and Blood of Christ the Son of God, the Priest begins this final dialogue- prayer with the People.

Priest: Through him, and with him, and in him,
O God, almighty Father,
in the unity of the Holy Spirit,
all glory and honor is yours,
for ever and ever.
People: Amen.

22. I thought we were about to receive Communion. Why are things suddenly going in slow motion?

THE COMMUNION RITE

BECAUSE this is so great an event, a mystery of the greatest proportions, we say special prayers and take particular actions to prepare us for receiving Jesus. Let's review a little of why this is such a momentous part of the Mass. As a devout Jewish person Jesus often celebrated the Passover meal. This was a very special Jewish feast. It commemorated and gave thanks for God's intervention which saved the lives of the first born sons of the Israelites and eventually all enslaved in Egypt. Throughout Jewish history this feast was celebrated once a year. Shortly before Jesus' passion and death he participated in the Passover with his Apostles.

Today we refer to that as The Last Supper. In addition to the usual ritual meal, Jesus added something that would change history forever. He *took* the bread and wine, *blessed* them and said "This is my body" and "This is my blood." Then he *broke* the bread and *shared* it with the Apostles saying to them, "Do this in memory of me."

From then on the Apostles, later the disciples and early Christians, all those down through the centuries until today, have continued to "Do this in memory of (Jesus)." According to the Catholic faith the words, 'Do this in memory of me,' have a far deeper meaning than just to remember someone or an event. Like our Hebrew ancestors we understand that this command of Jesus means 'bring this back to actually happening again in the here and now.' Today this is what we call the Mass. Acting in the person of Christ, the priest will *take, bless, break and share* the bread and wine. As he says the words that Jesus spoke at The Last Supper these gifts will become the Body and Blood of Jesus. When we receive the Body and Blood of Jesus Christ we too are changed forever in order that we might change the world.

We've just described this part of the Mass in the previous section. Following this Eucharistic Prayer then, the Communion Rite is the part of our worship in which we gather as a family at the table of the Lord to receive the one Body and Blood of Jesus Christ. As we receive the Eucharist we are nourished as one People, the one Body of Christ. As Catholic Christians we believe in the Real Presence, that the Body and Blood of Jesus Christ are truly present in the Holy Communion which we receive. We believe that in receiving Communion we are fed by Christ, nourished and healed by Christ and become Christ for the world. As St. Augustine said and Pope Francis has recently echoed: "We become what we receive."

During The Communion Rite we'll stand at certain times to gather as a family. At other times we'll kneel to express adoration and our own humility in the Presence of Jesus. We will also maintain a profound, sacred and prayerful silence after consuming the Body and Blood of Jesus.

The Priest will lead the People through the following prayers and gestures:

The Lord's Prayer
The Rite of Peace
Breaking of the Bread - The Fraction Rite and the Lamb of God
The Invitation to Communion and the Reception of Communion
The Purification
The Prayer after Communion

All of these separate prayers and gestures, described in the next sections, combine to prepare us as a family for the amazing gift of receiving the Body and Blood of Jesus Christ.

23. Finally, the part that begins the wonderful, communal "at home with family" feeling.

THE LORD'S PRAYER

THIS is perhaps the most widely known prayer in the world by people of many faiths. It makes people feel like we are all family. Some Christians consider it to be the best summary of the whole gospel. At a certain point during Jesus' time here on earth with us, the Apostles saw him praying and asked him: Lord, teach us to pray. (Matthew 6:9-15; Luke 11:1-4) Jesus' response to them formed the prayer we still say today. For that reason we call this prayer The Lord's Prayer. People usually refer to this prayer as the Our Father, using the first words as the title.

There are four parts of this special time of family prayer:

> the invitation to pray, the prayer, the embolism (a short prayer inserted by the priest) and the doxology (the concluding prayer of praise to the Trinity).

The Priest begins this time of family prayer by inviting the People to pray with these words:

> *At the Savior's command*
> *and formed by divine teachings,*
> *we dare to say:"*

As we say or sing this prayer at Mass we all stand together and sometimes hold hands, signifying a family gathered as one to address "our" father. It succinctly and beautifully makes seven basic requests of *"Our Father Who art in heaven*

> *-- hallowed be thy name*
> *-- thy kingdom come*
> *-- thy will be done*
>   *on earth as it is in heaven*
> *-- give us this day our daily bread, and*
> *-- forgive us our trespasses*
>   *as we forgive those who trespass against us*
> *-- lead us not into temptation, but*
> *-- deliver us from evil"*

The Priest then continues alone what is called the embolism (a short interlude prayer):

> *"Deliver us, Lord, we pray, from every evil,*
> *graciously grant peace in our days,*
> *that, by the help of your mercy,*
> *we may be always free from sin*
> *and safe from all distress,*
> *as we await the blessed hope*
> *and the coming of our Savior, Jesus Christ."*

The People respond with a prayerful and well known doxology:

> *"For the kingdom,*
> *the power and the glory are yours*
> *now and for ever."*

This particular line is well known by many Protestant Christians who have always said it as part of the Our Father prayer. Only in recent times have the Catholics said this additional line when praying the Our Father during the Mass. Outside of Mass it's still not added on to the Our Father by most Catholic Christians. It's not referenced in the gospel of Matthew or Luke. It was prayed by early Christians, and so it's considered to be part of the prayers of the Church from earliest times.

All Christians know the Our Father by heart. People from many other faiths are also very familiar with it. In recent translations meant to refresh the prayers of the Mass to their original wordings, the Our Father was not changed at all. The reason for no change at that time was precisely because it is so widely known throughout the world.

24. We all love this part because we can be natural but what does it mean?

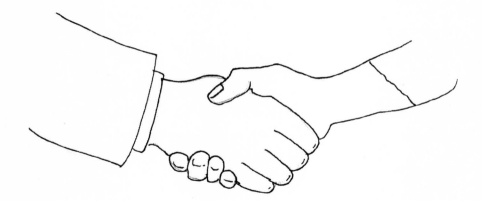

AEK

THE RITE OF PEACE

After the Resurrection of Jesus he found the Apostles huddled in fear behind locked doors. He came and stood among them greeting them with these words, "Peace be with you." (John 20:19) Jesus did not chastise them for their lack of faith, loyalty or courage. Rather he greeted them with love and mercy.

In this part of the Mass while the People are still standing together, the Priest prays:

> "Lord Jesus Christ, who said to your Apostles, Peace I leave you, my peace I give you, look not on our sins, but on the faith of your Church, and graciously grant her peace and unity in accordance with your will. Who live and reign for ever and ever."

The People respond with agreement to this prayer, by saying:

> "Amen."

We're asking Jesus once again for the peace of reconciliation. The first time we asked to be reconciled was during the Penitential Act near the beginning of the Mass. Then when we prayed the Creed together we were essentially saying "we stand with you God and with your Church." Now, before we receive the Body and Blood of Jesus Christ, we focus on our need for reconciliation with one another, with those standing right next to us as well as those among our families and friends with whom we need to be reconciled. We also are asking to be reconciled with everyone in the human family including strangers we have avoided in the past.

This gesture to express peace to one another was seen as a common sign of love, comfort and joy among the early Christians which we read in several of Paul's epistles: 1 Cor 16:20; 2 Cor 13:12; Rom 16:16; 1 Thess 5:26. *Greet one another with a holy kiss.*

And among those with whom we are at odds, we read in: 1 John 4:19-21: *If anyone says "I love God," but hates his brother, he is a liar.*

Finally in the Gospel of Matthew (5:23-24) we read: *Therefore, if you bring your gift to the altar, and there recall that your brother has anything against you, leave your gift there at the altar, go first and be reconciled with your brother, and then come and offer your gift.*

This Rite of Peace is meant to be an offering of peace on many levels. We who are gathered as a family during the Mass are offering each other "the peace of Christ." We're acting as Christ did with the Apostles in the Upper Room. We're sharing our joy with those among us because we all believe that Jesus is now present with us.

Secondly, we often never know what inner turmoil those standing next to us are experiencing but we can offer each other the peace of Christ which is greater than any worldly gift we have to give.

We can also think of those among our families and friends who are not present but with whom we have unsettled relationships. In that case, we can silently pray for forgiveness and help from God to reconcile.

Finally, as we offer our gesture of peace we can have in mind those in the world whom we ignore, discriminate against or even denigrate. Here we can ask God's forgiveness and help to reconcile our hearts to love always.

With all this in mind, we hear the Priest say:

"The Peace of the Lord be with you always."

We begin our response by offering this same peace to the Priest:

And with your spirit."

Then the Priest suggests the following:

"Let us offer each other a sign of peace."

Let us remember the many layered purpose of our gesture as we reach out our hands to those around us saying:

"The peace of Christ be with you."

This Rite was one of the additions to the Liturgy of the Eucharist as a result of the changes following the Vatican Council II. As many of those changes, it was intended to bring back the gestures and prayers of the earliest Christians. The first process included the Priest coming down from the sanctuary and offering peace to some in the Assembly who then passed that message around. Later this was adjusted so that the Priest would stay in the sanctuary, offering peace to those few around him. This allowed for the prayer gesture to be offered by the People. The People already have the gift of peace and the responsibility through Baptism to bring Christ's peace to all the world.

*25. Why does the priest make such a
     show of breaking the bread and
     putting a small piece into the wine?*

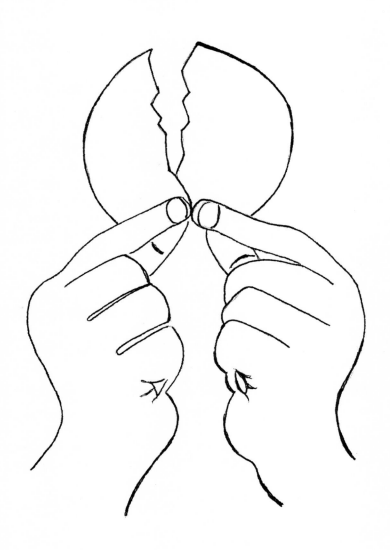

Breaking of the Bread /
The Fraction Rite and the Lamb of God

THIS is one of those moments in the Mass that goes by so quickly you might miss it and yet it has an extremely powerful message for us. In the Breaking of the Bread, also known as the Fraction Rite, the People participate in a short yet powerful gesture and prayer along with the Priest. It begins immediately after the Sign of Peace is exchanged. The priest takes the bread, now the Body of Christ, breaks it over the paten and places a small piece into the cup. As he does this he prays quietly.

"May this mingling of the Body and Blood
of our Lord Jesus Christ
bring eternal life to us who receive it."

Then he continues to break the one large piece of bread into small pieces preparing for distribution to everyone in attendance.

The first part of this gesture, when a fraction of the bread is added to the wine, symbolizes several things. It reminds us of Jesus' humanity and divinity as being one. It also recalls the rejoining of Jesus body and spirit in the Resurrection and reminds us of the promise we have of this same resurrection. In addition, the co-mingling of Jesus' Body and Blood is an overall symbol of unity.

The second part of this gesture, when the whole larger piece of bread is broken into smaller pieces, can offer us the suggestion of our own brokenness and need for God. As we grow in faith we realize more fully that it is only in our brokenness that we become aware of our need for God. Listening to the sound of the bread as it's breaking can provide a moment of meaningful prayer about this. Finally the breaking of the bread is meant to symbolize that we are all part of one body. We'll all be eating from the same bread and drinking from the same cup of wine.

During this time the People are still standing in unity with one another and singing the Lamb of God. This is a prayer based on words taken from the Gospel of John 1:29 when John the Baptist first greeted the approaching Jesus. Just before this we had made peace with our brothers and sisters and now we're identifying ourselves as sinners in need of salvation in this prayer. We're praying in the hope of making peace with God. Each line ends with our humble plea to God for mercy and then for peace, reminiscent of the story of the prodigal son (Luke 15:11-32). We might think of this as a prayer for reconciliation.

> *"Lamb of God, you take away the sins of the world,*
> *have mercy on us.*
> *Lamb of God, you take away the sins of the world,*
> *have mercy on us.*
> *Lamb of God, you take away the sins of the world,*
> *grant us peace."*

26. Why is this short invitation turned into such a big dramatic moment?

The Invitation to Communion
and the Reception of Communion

DID you ever have something wonderful about to happen in your life but the closer it gets the more you try to buy time, to put it off a little, to savor the expectation a little longer precisely because you're so excited about it or you think maybe you're not ready for that moment to happen? This is something like what happens here. We see ourselves as still not ready for the amazing experience of receiving the Body and Blood of Christ. And so, we pray to prepare.

After the "Lamb of God" the Assembly kneels once more to prepare for Communion. The reception of Communion begins with the Priest leading the People through the preparation. First, he begins to prepare himself by praying quietly:

> *"Lord Jesus Christ, Son of the living God,*
> *who, by the will of the Father*
> *and the work of the Holy Spirit,*
> *through your Death gave life to the world,*
> *free me by this, your most holy Body and Blood,*
> *from all my sins and from every evil;*
> *keep me always faithful to your commandments,*
> *and never let me be parted from you."*

or *"May the receiving of your Body and Blood,*
> *Lord Jesus Christ,*
> *not bring me to judgment and condemnation,*
> *but through your loving mercy*
> *be for me protection in mind and body*
> *and a healing remedy."*

After this prayer the Priest genuflects before the altar, takes the host into his hands and holds it slightly above the chalice. He invites the people to recognize and acclaim Jesus as truly present. Once again this prayer is drawn from the words of John the Baptist (John 1:29). In the final line of this prayer the Priest reminds us with words from Revelation 19:9 how blessed we are to be invited to receive such a gift.

> *"Behold the Lamb of God,*
> *behold him who takes away the sins of the world.*
> *Blessed are those called to the supper of the Lamb."*

The Priest joins the People in the response:

> *"Lord, I am not worthy*
> *that you should enter under my roof,*
> *but only say the word and my soul shall be healed."*

This response is a very poignant statement originally made by the Roman centurion who asked Jesus to heal the centurion's ailing servant. When Jesus offered to come to his house, the centurion said he was not worthy for Jesus to come under his roof. He insisted that it would be enough for Jesus just to say a word of healing right there on the road. Jesus said "in no one of Israel have I found such faith." (Matt 8:5-8, 10). When we say the words of the Roman centurion it becomes a reminder for us that we also are unworthy. It helps us to approach the reception of Communion with great humility. To ask Jesus for just one word to heal us is also an act of faith in the great healing power of Jesus that we too say will be enough to heal us.

After saying this short prayer together, the Priest himself prays quietly before consuming the Body of Christ.

> *"May the Body of Christ*
> *keep me safe for eternal life."*

The Priest then quietly says a second similar prayer before consuming the Blood of Christ:

> *"May the Blood of Christ*
> *keep me safe for eternal life."*

After this the People will process as one body toward the altar to receive the Body and Blood of Jesus Christ. This is the fourth time there is a procession during the Mass. At the beginning the Priest, Deacon, lector and altar servers processed in our name to signify that we are a pilgrim people journeying on the way home to God. The second time, the Priest processed with the Book of the Gospels to read from the word of God. The third time some from the Assembly processed to the altar to present the gifts in the name of the whole people. This time we all process as a family going to share at the table together.

As each person comes to the front of the procession the Priest or a Eucharistic Minister will hold up the host and say:

"The Body of Christ."

Before receiving and consuming the Body of Christ, each person replies with one word which signifies that he or she agrees with that statement and believes this is truly the Body of Christ.

"Amen."

The same process is repeated as we receive the Blood of Jesus Christ. The cup is presented with these words:

"The Blood of Christ."

Before receiving and consuming the Blood of Christ from the cup, we each respond:

Amen."

When the Priest is assisted in distributing Communion by a Deacon or Extraordinary Ministers of Holy Communion from the Assembly (often referred to as Eucharistic Ministers) this is not just for the sake of efficiency. It also reminds the People that we all are Church and that by Baptism we all share in the priesthood of Jesus. That means even as unordained priests we're all responsible and able to bring holiness to others.

What we witness happening in this part of the Mass is a very solemn moment of faith for all participants. This is when the Priest, the Deacon, the People all give their assent to the Real Presence of Jesus in the sacrament of the Eucharist. We're all saying that we believe the Body and Blood of Jesus Christ is truly present in the bread and wine which we're sharing. This is the greatest faith statement we ever make.

We've been part of this whole process. We saw the Priest *take* the bread at the Presentation of the gifts, *bless* it as he said the Eucharistic Prayer, *break* it during the Fraction rite and is now preparing to *share* it with all assembled. This combination of actions: *take, bless, break, and share* we know is reminiscent of Jesus' actions at the Last Supper (Luke 22:19). This was also the case with the disciples on the road to Emmaus after the resurrection. They walked and listened to Jesus without knowing it was him until he joined them for a meal. When "he took bread, said the blessing, broke it, and gave it to them" they recognized Jesus in "the breaking of the bread" (Luke 24:30-31). This was actually one of the first names given to what we today call the Mass. In the breaking of the bread we recognize Jesus as God, as our Teacher, our Healer, our Savior.

We might consider these four words in another way: *take, bless, break, share*. This is actually the life process we must go through in order to grow deeper in our relationship with God. At Baptism, *God took us* as heirs of heaven and *we were blessed* with many gifts. Through the course of our lives, *various challenges have broken our pride* and caused us to learn that *in giving/ sharing ourselves* is when we receive what we truly need. Each time we receive Communion we have an opportunity to be reminded of this constant life lesson and to choose growth again.

We also believe that when we receive the Eucharist we become the Eucharist. By consuming Jesus we become Jesus, as he said: "Whoever eats my flesh and drinks my blood remains in me and I in him" (John 6:56). Jesus said to the Apostles at the Last Supper "Do this in memory of me." And they have passed this on to many generations including our own today. To "do this" does not just mean to celebrate the Mass together. It also means what Jesus said to us: "Come you who are blessed by my Father. Inherit the kingdom prepared for you from the foundation of the world. . . .For I say to you, whatever you did for one of the least of my brethren, you did for me" (Matt 25:34, 40). We are being called by Jesus to live as he did in our current world, to bring his message of love to everyone in our lives today. We are called to be Christ in the world.

During the reception of Communion it is customary for the People to sing a song of unity, expressing our oneness as the Body of Christ. This reflects the prayer of Jesus for us and the actual reality that is happening. We're each becoming Christ. And as a community we're together becoming the Body of Christ.

Each time we receive Communion this becomes a little bit more true in our lives. We grow into our role as "Christ in the world," little by little. And the frailty and brokenness of our humanity becomes more and more healed. In the prayer said quietly by the Priest at the beginning of this part of the Mass we see these beautiful words:

> *"May the receiving of your Body and Blood,*
>
> *Lord Jesus Christ,*
>
> *not bring me to judgment and condemnation,*
>
> *but through your loving mercy*
>
> *be for me protection in mind and body*
>
> *and a healing remedy."*

Each time we receive the Body and Blood of Christ our human frailty experiences healing and we are then able to become more Christ-like. We are filled with God's grace, God's spirit to re-enter our lives and try to make Christ known to all.

27. A time to reflect:
How can we keep these good thoughts and feelings alive?

Purification and the Prayer after Communion

OFTEN we read in the Bible of the people's "fear of God." Scripture scholars of today tell us that what is trying to be expressed by the word "fear" is more what we would call "awe." God is far beyond what we can even imagine, a mystery unlimited. It's this sense of awe and respect for the mystery that causes us to treat all that is connected to Jesus with great care.

After everyone has received Communion the Priest, Deacon or an ordained Acolyte purifies the paten, the chalice and all other sacred vessels that have held the Body and Blood of Christ. This is preferably done at a side table. Because of the sacred use of these vessels great care is taken with them. Later the same special care will be taken to clean the altar linens as well. All of this reflects our wish to honor and respect Jesus who has come into our midst.

While performing the purification of the sacred vessels the Priest says quietly:

> "What has passed our lips as food, O Lord,
> may we possess in purity of heart,
> that what has been given to us in time
> may be our healing for eternity."

The People are seated during this important time and when the Priest is finished with the purification he too returns to sit in the presidential chair. This is a period of time sometimes referred to as a sacred silence. This allows both the Priest and the People to have time for personal prayer in thanksgiving for the great gift of the Eucharist. It may for some be a time to ask for the grace to continue to grow. In some parishes there is a reflective psalm sung or other music played during this time.

After some length of time the Priest stands and addresses the People:

> "Let us pray."

The People stand and as we did before the Opening Prayer of the Mass, we each form our own prayer silently. After a moment the Priest then says, in our names: The Prayer after Communion. This prayer is different at every Mass and reflects the particular theme of each liturgy. It will express in some way our gratitude for receiving the great gift of the Eucharist and ask that it may bear fruit in our daily lives and lead us into eternity.

The People respond to this prayer with agreement by saying:

"Amen."

28. *This last message is so short yet so very powerful.*

BE the Church

Care for the Poor. **Forgive often.**

Comfort the Afflicted. Turn from revenge.

Fight for the Powerless.

Shelter the Homeless. *Show Gratitude to All.*

Provide equal education. Protect the environment.

Assist those who are mentally ill.

Visit the sick and imprisoned.

Bring Peace to every Space and Person.

THE CONCLUDING RITE / THE DISMISSAL

THE Concluding Rite is quite short but very important. It might not seem very spiritual but this is a time when necessary announcements are made as we begin to return to our practical worldly lives. Some themes will be about growth and service events within the parish. Sometimes there are practical things that must be addressed too and this might be the time. At some parishes they choose to do this before the liturgy starts and at other parishes this might be the chosen time.

After the announcements, there follows a dialogue of greeting between the Priest and the People much like what was done at the beginning of the liturgy although we feel very different now. We're changed somehow. The Priest stands and says:

"The Lord be with you"

With this greeting, the People rise together as a community and respond:

"And also with you."

The Priest then blesses the People with the Sign of the Cross, saying:

*"May almighty God bless you,
the Father, and the Son, and the Holy Spirit."*

The People trace the Sign of the Cross on themselves in acceptance of this blessing, and say:

"Amen."

The Deacon or the Priest will dismiss the People, saying:

	"Go forth, the Mass is ended."
or	*"Go and announce the Gospel of the Lord."*
or	*"Go in peace, glorifying the Lord by your life."*
or	*"Go in Peace to love and serve the Lord and all his people."*
or	*"Go in Peace."*

The People reply:

"Thanks be to God."

The "dismissal" which this final dialogue of prayer is called is the source of the word Mass which we use today to describe the total liturgy. For many centuries the words for this were said in Latin: *"Ite missa est ."* This translates to: "Go, you are dismissed" meaning "you are sent" or we might say "you are missioned," or "you are sent on a mission." So, when we say we are going to Mass we might be saying, without knowing it, that we are going to Mass in order to be sent on a mission.

This is where the name for our liturgy came from. It's the purpose of the Mass. We go to praise, glorify and thank God. We ask to be fed and healed and nourished in order to continue God's work on earth. And the Priest, in the person of Christ, sends us forth with that small but powerful command: GO. This is how Jesus sent his Apostles into the world. "Go, therefore, and make disciples of all nations. . . ." (Matt 28:19a). This might actually be quite a frightening challenge to us if Jesus had not also added: "And behold, I am with you always, until the end of the age." (Matt 28:20b)

When we hear the words that commission us to "go forth" we say "Thanks be to God." As kids, many of us thought we were saying: Hooray, now I can go out and play again. Actually what we're expressing is our gratitude for being chosen through Baptism. How blessed we are to be the people God has commissioned to bring Christ to the world. We're being asked at the conclusion of each Mass to continue the work of converting the world to love. And we're expressing our gratefulness to be chosen.

After our response of "Thanks be to God," the Priest kisses the altar and makes a profound bow before this sacred place which held the Body and Blood of Jesus Christ. The Priest then moves around the altar and with all the others who assisted him, he makes a final bow to the altar as they begin the final procession.

As the final procession, with the cross leading the way, moves from the altar out to the street, once again we are a People on the move. Like the Hebrews in their Exodus, like the Apostles to all parts of the earth, we are going out to our world to do the work of Jesus who has sent us. We no longer carry the Book of Gospels with us because the word of God is within us now as is the Body and Blood of Jesus Christ. It's our mission now to bring Christ to the world.

As Fr. David McBriar, OFM, a priest serving the Raleigh diocese, once said: *"If we are here celebrating Mass today because we believe in and want to follow Jesus of Nazareth, then there is only one question to ask: What does the world need and how can I help?"*

29. Inspirational Quotes for "Going forth" to keep the spirit of Jesus alive.

(taken from 100s of holy cards, song books, prayer books and the Bible)

"In virtue of their baptism, all the members of the People of God have become missionary disciples." *(Pope Francis, The Joy of the Gospel 120, Matthew 28:19)*

"Whoever wishes to be great among you shall be your servant; the Son of Man did not come to be served, but to serve." *(Matthew 21:26, 28)*

Jesus said to them again, "Peace be with you. As the Father sent me, so I send you." *(John 20:21)*

"The lay people form the core of the community that will act as a leaven for others." *(Pope Emeritus Benedict XVI: Pastoral Convention, Rome 2009)*

"Sanctity does not consist especially in doing extraordinary things, but in allowing God to act through our weakness and the strength of his grace." *(Pope Francis, General Audience, 10-13-13)*

"We must make the kind of society where it is easier for people to be good." *(Peter Maurin, Co-Founder of the Catholic Worker)*

"We need to focus our community's energy in order to transform the parish into a culture where discipleship is normal to all." *(Pope St. John Paul II, General Audience 1980)*

"Every Christian is a missionary to the extent that he or she has encountered the love of God in Christ Jesus." *(Pope Francis, The Joy of the Gospel 120)*

"Christianity without discipleship is always Christianity without Christ." *(Dietrich Bonhoeffer, The Cost of Discipleship)*

"The Church which 'goes forth' is a community of missionary disciples who take the first step, who are involved and supportive, who bear fruit and rejoice." *(Pope Francis, The Joy of the Gospel, 24)*

"See these Christians how they love one another." *(A saying attributed to non-Christians from the earliest century of Christianity)*

"For the Christian there is no such thing as a "stranger." There is only the neighbor...the person near us and needing us." *(St. Edith Stein)*

"Lord, teach me to serve you as you deserve...To give and not to count the cost...To labor and ask for no reward...." *(attributed to St. Ignatius Loyola)*

"Whenever our interior life becomes caught up in its own interests and concerns, there is no longer room for others, no place for the poor." *(Pope Francis, The Joy of the Gospel, 2)*

"Preach the Gospel at all times and, when necessary, use words." *(attributed to St. Francis Assisi)*

"God did not tell us to follow Him because He needed our help, but because He knew that loving Him would make us whole." *(St. Irenaeus)*

"You have been told what is good and what the Lord requires of you: only to do right, to love goodness, and to walk humbly with your God." *(Micah 6:8)*

"For this is the message you have heard from the beginning. . . Children, let us love not in word or speech but in deed and truth." *(1 John 3:11, 18)*

"Do you know, what I have done for you, you who call me your Teacher and your Lord? If I have washed your feet, so you must do what I have done for you." *(from hymn "Song of the Lord's Command" by David Haas inspired by John 13:12-15)*

"In all places and circumstances, Christians, with the help of their pastors, are called to hear the cry of the poor." *(Pope Francis, The Joy of the Gospel, 191)*

"I see in my neighbor the person of Jesus Christ." *(St. Gerard Majella)*

"Actions speak louder than words. Let your words teach and your actions speak." *(St. Anthony of Padua)*

"God has no need for your mercy, but the poor have." *(St. Augustine)*

"It is to those who have the most need of us that we ought to share our love more especially." *(St. Francis de Sales)*

"By this everyone will know that you are my disciples, that you love one another." *(John 13:35)*

"Christ has no body now on earth but yours; no hands but yours; no feet but yours. Yours are the eyes through which the compassion of Christ must look out on the world. Yours are the feet with which He is to go about doing good. Yours are the hands with which He is to bless His people." *(St. Teresa of Avila)*

"Extend your mercy toward others, so that there can be no one in need whom you meet without helping." *(St. Vincent de Paul)*

"God does not look so much at the greatness of our actions, nor even at their difficulty, but at the love with which we do them." *(St. Therese of Lisieux)*

"I believe that I was created to share my life and my love with God and other people forever, and that God created the things of this world only to help me achieve this goal." *(St. Ignatius Loyola)*

"Whoever welcomes you welcomes me, and whoever welcomes me welcomes the one who sent me." *(Matthew 10:40)*

"Father, you created me and put me on earth for a purpose. Jesus, you died for me and called me to complete your work. Holy Spirit, help me to carry out the work for which I was created and called." *(Fr. Bernard Bassett, S.J.)*

"We were determined to share with you not only the gospel of God, but our very selves as well. . . ." *(1 Thessalonians 2:8a)*

"Jesus chose to minister to the least, the lost and the last. Grant me, O Lord, to see everyone now with new eyes." *(St. Ignatius Loyola)*

"This is the first obligation of being a disciple – telling others about Jesus by our lives and our words." *(Christine M. Fletcher in her book 24/7 Christian)*

"Always be ready to give an explanation to anyone who asks for a reason for your hope." *(1 Peter 3:15)*

"If we are here celebrating Mass today because we believe in and want to follow Jesus of Nazareth, then there is only one question to ask: What does the world need and how can I help?" *(Fr. David McBriar, OFM –Raleigh diocese)*

"Follow me and I will make you fishers of men." *(Jesus in the Gospel of Mark 1:17)*

"We need to recognize ourselves as sinners who need God's mercy and forgiveness. We need to love and forgive others." *(Christine M. Fletcher in her book 24/7 Christian)*

"Go, sell what you have, and give to the poor and you will have treasure in heaven: then come follow me." *(Mark 10:21b)*

"Even those who do not know God sometimes recognize God in the presence of a truly religious person, happening or event. Suddenly they say "There is God." *(Louis Evely in his book Our Prayer)*

"For it is in giving that we receive. . . ." *(St. Francis Assisi)*

"Do not neglect hospitality, for through it some have unknowingly entertained angels." *(Hebrews 13:2)*

"Every Christian is to become another Christ." *(C.S. Lewis in Mere Christianity)*

"We have to forget ourselves long enough to lend a helping hand." *(Philippians 2:4)*

"Sufferings gladly bourne for others convert more people than sermons." *(St. Therese of Lisieux)*

"You are the salt of the earth. . . .You are the light of the world. . . .your light must shine before others, that they may see your good deeds and glorify your heavenly Father." *(Matthew 5:13a, 14a,16)*

"Let us be renewed by God's mercy. . .and let us become agents of this mercy, channels through which God can water the earth, protect all creation and make justice and peace flourish." *(Pope Francis)*

"Do nothing out of selfishness or out of vainglory; rather, humbly regard others as more than yourselves. . . .Have among yourselves the same attitude that is also yours in Christ Jesus. . . ." *(Philippians 2:3, 5)*

Finally, all of you, be of one mind, sympathetic, loving toward one another, compassionate, humble. . .a blessing for others, because to this you were called. . ." *(1 Peter 3:8, 9b)*

"Blessed be the God and Father of our Lord Jesus Christ, the Father of compassion and God of all encouragement, who encourages us in our every affliction, so that we may be able to encourage those who are in any affliction. . . . *(2 Corinthians 1:3-4)*

"Loving God of the morning, you spread the table of your love before me this day. May my heart be wide open, grateful and ready to welcome you in those I meet today." *(St. John Henry Cardinal Newman)*

"It is only with the heart that one sees rightly. What is essential is invisible to the eye." *(Antoine de Saint-Exupery in The Little Prince)*

"It's not so much that the Church of Christ has a mission, as that the mission of Jesus Christ has a Church." *(Fr. James Mallon in Divine Renovation)*

"And now I (Jesus) will no longer be in the world. As you (Father) sent me into the world, so I sent them into the world." *(John 17:11a, 18)*

"In the evening of life we shall be judged by Love." *(St. John of the Cross)*

"Go, therefore, and make disciples of all nations. . . . And behold, I am with you always, until the end of the age." *(Matthew 28:19a, 20b)*

THE CORPORAL WORKS OF MERCY

To feed the hungry
To give drink to the thirsty
To clothe the naked
To shelter the homeless
To care for the sick
To visit the imprisoned
To bury the dead

THE SPIRITUAL WORKS OF MERCY

To instruct those in need of learning
To counsel the doubtful
To redirect sinners
To forgive offences willingly
To comfort the afflicted
To bear wrongs patiently
To pray for the living and the dead

(This current listing of the Works of Mercy is based on the Gospel of Matthew chapter 25 and various Old Testament passages.)

30. The parts of our Catholic Liturgical Calendar

Advent   * Christmas Time*   *Ordinary Time*

Lent   *Easter Time*

ADVENT

ACCORDING to the Catholic Liturgical Calendar of the Catholic Church the Liturgical Year begins in late November or early December at the start of Advent. The word *advent* refers to *the coming*. For Christians this represents a looking forward, a preparing, a waiting for God to enter this human world. It's the time in which we celebrate God's presence in the past, the future and the present days of our lives.

The great Doctor of the Church, Saint Bernard of Clairvaux (1090-1153) once wrote about Advent this way:

> *"We know that there are three comings of the Lord. In the first coming he was seen here on earth among us. In the last coming he will be seen in glory and majesty. The intermediate coming lies between the other two, like a road on which we travel from the first coming to the last."*

The First and Second Sundays of Advent focus on the future coming of Christ. The Third Sunday's focus is on the present coming of Christ into our daily lives. The focus of the Fourth Sunday is on the birth of Jesus, the historical past event. When you listen carefully to the weekly readings and prayers you can hear these themes.

At this time of the year we rejoice with gratitude for the great loving promise of God to send a messiah to his chosen people. And we celebrate the awesome event of Jesus' birth, God coming into our humanity. Yet, the most important part of Advent is for us to prepare ourselves to live our gift of faith even more actively. It's not enough for us to celebrate the Eucharist each Sunday together. It's not enough for us to think of God occasionally and pray for our requests. As Pope Francis has asked us, we must move outside the walls of our church and become active Christians in the world. We're meant to do more than just go to church but rather to BE Church, bringing Christ into every action of our lives. When each of us adds Christ's light to the world we have fleshed out God a bit more. And this is how we truly spread the joy of Christmas.

CHRISTMAS TIME

OBSERVING all the physical evidence around us, Christmas Time seems to start around Thanksgiving and lasts until December 25th. All the preparation, all the joy, fun, partying, celebration, gift-giving are over by the end of the day on 12/25.

Yet in our Catholic spiritual tradition Christmas is only beginning on the 25th of December. The prelude to our Christmas Time starts with Advent. This is our time of spiritual preparation for celebrating the past, future and present coming of God into our human experience.

Then on December 25th we begin the full celebration of Christmas. And it's not just a one-day event. For us it will last for almost three weeks. During these weeks which we call Christmas Time we'll celebrate many great feasts.

On the First Sunday following Christmas Day we celebrate the Feast of The Holy Family of Jesus, Mary and Joseph. In the Scriptural readings for this feast we hear many guidelines on how to be loving within our families including our church family and our world family. The Holy Family is honored with this special feast and held up to us as a model of love and respect for us to follow.

Then on the first day of the new year we celebrate the Solemnity of Mary, the Holy Mother of God. On this feast we're reminded in a special way of the amazing part that Mary played in the whole story of Christmas. It was with Mary's "yes" to God's invitation that the Christmas story began. Not only are we immensely grateful for Mary's faithful love of God but she provides us with yet another example of how to live our Christian lives. Listening for God's call in each day and responding with our "yes" is what Mary's example shows us about true faith in action.

The Second Sunday after Christmas is dedicated to the Solemnity of The Epiphany of the Lord. This is a well known feast that sometimes used to be called "Little Christmas." In some cultures Christmas was not actually celebrated until this day. The cultural development of this had to do with the idea that this was the day on which the rest of the world, beyond just the Hebrew community, first learned of Jesus. The word *"epiphany"* means "manifestation," or a showing. The significance is God showing in human form to all the world. The Feast of the Three Kings is another name for this day since it commemorates the visit and adoration of Jesus by the wise men (the magi) from the East. They represent this "outside world" of which we are a part. One of the messages that this feast carries is that Jesus, the Messiah of Israel and Son of God, has come as Savior for *the whole world*. The wise men who offered gifts also become the model for our gift-giving to each other. They give us the example of how we should each offer our most valuable gifts to God.

The Third Sunday after Christmas is the final day of the Church's Christmas Time. It is the Feast of the Baptism of the Lord and marks the beginning of Jesus' public life. After Jesus is baptized by John the Baptist in the Jordan River, the sky opens and a voice from heaven proclaims "This is my beloved Son, with whom I am well pleased." (Matthew 3:17) With that divine declaration, the beginning of Jesus' story is now complete. With those words we again have a manifestation of *Emmanuel,* God with us, and a foreshadowing of what is to come.

ORDINARY TIME

THIS reference of time on the Liturgical Calendar is anything but "ordinary." This word is used to designate the Sundays not reserved for special Solemnities or Feasts. The Church uses *ordinal* numbers to count these days, all of which together are called *Ordinary Time*. For example: Second Sunday in Ordinary Time or Eighteenth Sunday in Ordinary Time. Altogether there are Thirty-Four Sundays in Ordinary Time though the calendar varies from year to year so not all of them are used each year.

The first part of Ordinary Time, runs from the end of Christmas Time to the beginning of Lent. During this period most of the Gospel readings proclaim Jesus' work of preaching, and healing and of his lessons and miracles or signs to increase faith. We get a picture of Jesus calling the Apostles and then traveling with them to various areas teaching and healing the people.

The closer we come to Lent, the more we hear of what is unfolding between Jesus and the powerful people who are beginning to plot against him. Even as his teaching and miracles draw crowds of people to follow him, those in power among the Jewish hierarchy become more threatened by this influence he is showing within the community as a whole. Something must be done. This first part of Ordinary Time will stop temporarily when Lent begins on Ash Wednesday.

The second part of Ordinary Time resumes after the great feast of Pentecost which comes 50 days after the feast of Easter. Throughout the Summer months the Gospel will proclaim more about Jesus' teachings and miracles. The Second reading will often be from the book of Acts, telling us of the Apostles' and disciples' work in building up Christianity. During these weeks we hear Jesus teach and also hear the Apostles act on his teachings and his example to them. It's an interesting model for us: to hear Jesus' teachings and then see how his followers acted on what he said.

Finally, as Ordinary Time continues on through the Autumn months we will hear Jesus spending more time instructing those closest to him. He will be telling them what to expect in his final days as well as in theirs. Just as the beginning of Ordinary Time in January told us of the beginnings of Jesus mission, here we're told by Jesus of the end of his time on earth. This is when we hear proclaimed the need to die with Christ in order to live eternally with God. Jesus is giving this special group of followers the most significant instructions on how to carry on his work of preaching and healing to build the Kingdom of God on earth. We're also given the picture of how the Apostles find what Jesus is saying hard to understand and believe. Only later, after the Resurrection, will these words of Jesus give them a full sense of their calling.

LENT

LENT is a time for spiritual renewal and the focus for this renewal period is our Baptism. In the early 4th Century Constantine as the new Emperor of the reunited Roman Empire, decreed the end of persecution of Christians and the beginning of tolerance for Christianity. From this Edict of Milan in 313 and onward many and then almost all people throughout the Roman Empire converted to Christianity. The numbers were so great that this presented the Church with the challenge of developing a process for becoming a Christian which was eventually called the catechumenate (the teaching process). This early process of initiation was revived through the Second Vatican Council and is today known as the Rite of Christian Initiation of Adults (RCIA).

The original 4th Century catechumenate ended with a 40 day retreat of final spiritual preparation for initiation through the reception of Baptism, Confirmation and Eucharist. This 40 day preparation is still with us today in slightly different formats. Those in the RCIA process take part in a Rite of Election with the bishop and three Scrutiny Rites during the weeks before Baptism. In each parish church parishioners pray for the catechumens.

During this same time all parishioners throughout the whole Catholic Church are directed to observe 40 days of Prayer, Fasting, and Almsgiving.

While these three practices are followed at other times, everyone is asked to intensify them during this season as a way to prepare themselves for the renewal of their Baptismal promises on Easter.

Lent which began as a 40 day intense spiritual preparation for catechumens in the early Church eventually became a 40 day retreat for all Catholics.

The Gospel readings for Lent follow the Cycle that's appropriate each year unless there are catechumens in the parish. In this case, special readings are chosen to emphasize the conversion process of dying to self in order to live with Christ. The first two Sundays focus on Jesus, both in his intense spiritual preparation and in his glory. The next three Sundays focus on the journey of conversion necessary for all Christians.

To follow this process look over the themes for the Sundays of Lent listed below: (following the Readings for Cycle C)

First Sunday of Lent—Jesus is led by the Holy Spirit into the desert for forty days to be tempted and becomes strengthened through his resistance to temptation. (Luke 4:1-13)

Second Sunday of Lent—Jesus is transfigured in glory in the presence of Moses and Elijah, witnessed by the Apostles Peter, James and John (Luke 9:28b-36)

Third Sunday of Lent—The Samaritan woman at Jacob's well meets Jesus and moves gradually from total skeptic to missionary disciple for Jesus the Messiah (John 4:5-42). This very special Meeting of Jesus with this woman is the longest conversation Jesus shares with an individual recorded in all the Gospels. It is a dramatic and poignant description of the conversion process we all might experience.

Fourth Sunday of Lent—The man born blind who accepts physical healing and eventually makes a full spiritual commitment to Jesus as Messiah (John 9:1-41)

Fifth Sunday of Lent—The raising of Lazarus from the dead which challenges Martha, then Mary, to make an act of faith in Jesus as the one who will conquer death and bring us to Eternal Life (John 11:1-45)

Sixth Sunday of Lent—First before the Mass actually begins we hear a full or short Gospel reading telling of Jesus triumphal entry into Jerusalem. The Priest and other ministers process into the church while the People hold palm branches to celebrate this event.

Once the Mass has begun and at the usual time for the Gospel reading, the whole passion narrative is proclaimed. This dramatic recalling begins at the Last Supper with the institution of the Eucharist followed by Jesus' agony in the garden, his betrayal and arrest, his physical persecution, condemnation to death and crucifixion. We experience Jesus as giving his life for us as well as modeling his great love for us so that we follow this example in our lives. (Luke 22:14-23:56)

The last week of Lent is sometimes referred to as Holy Week or The Triduum which is described in this next section.

THE TRIDUUM

THIS is an unusual word but if you know how to say it (tri—du—um) you'll feel very smart. It simply means a three part event, in this case that would be Holy Thursday, Good Friday and the Easter Vigil. This grouping of liturgies is also commonly referred to by many Catholics as Holy Week.

On the morning of Holy Thursday the bishop of each diocese celebrates the Chrism Mass. In certain dioceses it is celebrated on a day earlier in that week for convenience. At this Mass three oils are blessed by the bishop and all the priests of the diocese and then distributed to each parish. These oils will be used in all the parishes throughout the year to anoint people receiving the sacraments. They are the Oil of Chrism, the Oil of Catechumens and the Oil of the Sick.

The Oil of Catechumens is used to anoint catechumens in preparation for baptism.

The Sacred Chrism is used for the anointing at Baptism, at Confirmation, and for the hands of priests as well as the heads of bishops at Ordination. These are all indelible sacraments received only once. This oil is also used for the dedication of new churches, altars and sacred vessels.

The Oil of the Sick is used during the Sacrament of Anointing the Sick.

The Chrism Mass is also a celebration of the Priesthood of Christ. On this day all the priests of a diocese who have gathered together with the bishop, all as one, concelebrate the Mass, bless the new oils and most importantly renew their priestly promises.

In the evening of Holy Thursday there is a celebration of the Last Supper when Jesus instituted the Eucharist. As the result of our Baptism we are now in community with Jesus. We are not only fed and nourished by Jesus but taught how we must follow him as we build the kingdom. We must follow the model as Jesus did in humble service to all others in our lives. This lesson is demonstrated as the priest washes the feet of twelve parishioners emulating Jesus who washed the feet of his twelve disciples.

The three sacred oils blessed earlier are presented to the Priest and will be used for the first time in Saturday's liturgy.

At the completion of this Mass the remaining Eucharist is removed in solemn procession to an altar of repose (a temporary location where adoration may take place). This Eucharist will be saved and received on the following day when there will be no Mass but simply distribution of Communion. The linen from the main altar is stripped, the tabernacle is left open and empty, and the sanctuary light is extinguished, all in commemoration of the passion and death of Jesus.

Good Friday is the day on which we remember that Jesus, after great torture and crucifixion, died for our salvation. The altar is bare, the tabernacle empty and there is no music or flowers. The Priest and Deacon prostrate themselves to signify our humble submission to Jesus for all he has sacrificed for us. We hear the Passion narrative from the Gospel according to

John. Then we process toward the bare altar to adore the cross with reverent touches or kisses, taking note of all the suffering Jesus went through for us. This instrument of torturous death is now the glorious symbol of our salvation. In Baptism we died with Christ to live with him eternally. Today in the quiet barrenness of this liturgy we reflect on those mysteries.

After the adoration of the cross, the Eucharist is brought from the altar of repose and offered to those present. This is the only day of the year when we receive Communion without there being a Mass of consecration. A previous title for the liturgy of this day was "the Mass of the pre-sanctified." Since there is actually no Mass that reference is no longer commonly used.

After all have received Communion the Priest, Deacon and People leave quietly on this day to commemorate Jesus' death.

Holy Saturday follows and the preparations are made for the greatest Church feast of the whole Liturgical Year -- Easter. This is the greatest feast because it celebrates the greatest

and most central belief of the faith – the Resurrection of Jesus from the dead. Each parish celebrates a Mass after sundown and then again on the following morning.

Sometime during the day the church is decorated with a profusion of flowers and new linens on the altar. Joyous music is prepared, lectors and cantors practice for the Scriptural proclamations. Many different liturgical ministers take on their roles for this great event. All is old—all is new—all is forever.

The liturgy begins outdoors after sundown. The Priest blesses a newly built fire, a new Paschal candle and then new light is passed on to all attending as small candles are lit and everyone processes into a darkened church.

Those assembled listen to Scriptural stories of our spiritual ancestors from thousands of years ago. The readings remind us of our on-going and eternal covenant with God. Mostly we hear that God, from the first days of creation, has always remained faithful to us, whether we ourselves were wandering away or faithfully close. To each reading we sing our responses of gratitude and humility from the book of Psalms. We also recite the great Litany of the Saints asking for prayers from our spiritual ancestors. They have all shared the same experience as humans and remained faithful examples for us, modeling our life's purpose—to become a saint.

All witness the Baptism of the catechumens and then renew our own baptismal promises—to believe in Christ and to act as Christ in the world. The catechumens and those Christians seeking full communion with the Catholic Church then receive Confirmation. Before all receive Communion these catechumens and candidates receive the Body and Blood of Jesus Christ for the first time. Each part of this liturgy is very moving for everyone gathered. This is the culmination of our 40 days of spiritual renewal throughout Lent and we celebrate: Jesus is Risen!

EASTER TIME

Do you think of Easter as a Season? Or do you suppose it's just one day, a night and a day – Saturday night and then Sunday? Or maybe you think of it as several days such as Passion/Palm Sunday, Holy Thursday, Good Friday, Holy Saturday, then Easter Sunday? At various times in history these were the customs – but not now.

Actually this liturgical Easter Time is celebrated as one feast lasting 50 days! It's celebrated from Easter Sunday throughout seven weeks (49 days) and then finally the 50th day is Pentecost, which in ancient Greek means 50th.

The designation of this timing originally grew out of the Jewish celebration of harvest at the end of the planting season begun at the time of Passover. In a sense Easter Time, culminating in Pentecost, symbolically represents the harvest of Jesus' life on earth. It also commemorates the beginning of Jesus' followers going forth to spread the seeds of good news, thereby increasing the harvest.

Each Sunday during Easter Time is referred to as a Sunday *of* Easter, not a Sunday *after* Easter. This is meant to signify that Easter is not just one Sunday but a significant Time that continues for all 50 days. The Church takes this time to celebrate, unfolding and sharing the full meaning of the great Paschal Mystery – the passion, dying and rising of Jesus Christ. This amazing series of events is the foundation of Christianity and the highest point of faith.

Imagine if the Resurrection had never taken place. There would be no basis on which to claim faith in Jesus Christ as the Son of God. Throughout these 50 days the Church presents the Paschal/Easter Mystery in many different ways. It unfolds the meaning of many symbols used in sacramental liturgies such as water, oil, light, joyful music, white garments, lilies, eggs – new life in many forms. During Easter Time all Scripture readings are taken from the New Testament reflecting the new covenant brought forth by Jesus Christ. There is a Church directive to receive the Eucharist during this Time, to take part in the highest and deepest expression of faith.

Easter Time ends on the Seventh Sunday which is the feast of Pentecost. Often referred to as the birthday of the church, this feast is the final event of Easter Time. It marks both an ending and the great beginning of the Holy Spirit's guidance to all believers missioned to be disciples throughout the world.

"Go, therefore, and make disciples of all nations. . . ."
(Matt 28:19)